INSIGHT COMPACT GUIDE

Dominican Republic

Compact Guide: Dominican Republic is the ideal quick-reference guide to this Caribbean paradise. It tells you all you need to know about the country's attractions, from the colonial splendors of Santo Domingo to sun-kissed, palm-fringed beaches, from the magic of forests and mountains to the musical beat of the *merengue*.

This is one of 120 Compact Guides, which combine the interests and enthusiasms of two of the world's best known information providers: Insight Guides, whose titles have set the standard for visual travel guides since 1970, and Discovery Channel, the world's premier source of nonfictio

GW00602678

Star Attractions

An instant reference to some of the Dominican Republic's most popular tourist attractions to help you on your way.

Santo Domingo Cathedral p21

The Malecón p28

Mercado Modelo p33

Museo de l'Hombre Dominicano p34

Jardín Botánico p36

Puerto Plata p40

Las Terrenas beach p44

Parque Nacional Jaragua p62

Lake Enriquillo p63

Enriquillo p64

Boca Chica beach p66

Dominican Republic

Introduction

Dominican Republic – Sweet Paradise **5**
Historical Highlights..**14**

Places

Route 1: Santo Domingo **18**
Route 2: Along the Amber Coast: Puerta Plata – Sosúa –
Río San Juan – Santa Bárbara de Semaná **39**
Route 3: On the Trail of Christopher Columbus: Puerta Plata –
La Isabela – Navarrete – Monte Cristi.........................**45**
Route 4: High Mountains and Fertile Valleys: Puerto Plata –
Santiago de los Caballeros – La Vega – Jarabacoa –
Constanza – Santo Domingo.......................................**49**
Route 5: The Southwest: Santo Domingo – San Cristóbal –
Nigua – Baní – Azua de Compostela – Barahona –
Pedernales **56**
Route 6: Around Lake Enriquillo: Barahona – Neiba –
Jimaní – Duvergé – Barahona......................................**63**
Route 7: From Sugar to Tourism: Santo Domingo – Boca
Chica – San Pedro de Macorís – La Romana **65**
Route 8: The Southeast: La Romana – Higüey –
Sabana de la Mar...**69**

Culture

A Diverse Heritage **73**
Festivals and Folklore **75**

Leisure

Food and Drink **77**
Active Holidays **80**

Practical Information

Getting There **83**
Getting Around **84**
Facts for the Visitor..**86**
Accommodation..**90**

Index **95**

Dominican Republic – Sweet Paradise

Columbus came here in search of gold and silver, but he also found what most of today's visitors come for: sea, sand and sun. Around 2 million tourists a year visit the land once known to the Taíno Indians as *Aíti* ('mountainous country'). Travel operators would love to call it plain *Dominicana*, because they feel 'Dominican Republic' doesn't sound Caribbean enough.

Boca Chica beach

The *República Dominicana* has everything one could ever hope to find in a tropical paradise. It's warm and sunny all year round, the coast is lined with magnificent beaches and palm tree groves, the interior contains luxuriant meadows, hilly landscapes, tobacco fields and sugar cane plantations, all framed against the unexpected backdrop of high mountains. The people are cheerful and friendly wherever you go. They have a great sense of color and a particular love of music: alongside more traditional refrains, the *merengue*, with its accompanying dance, can be heard all over the island.

Dense forest in the interior

This state of around 8 million people which shares the island of Hispaniola with the Republic of Haiti has made great efforts over the past few years to fulfill the expectations of visitors from abroad. A construction boom has produced a series of hotels and holiday villages; the infrastructure has been improved; and the old part of the capital, Santo Domingo, was given a face-lift in time for the 500th anniversary of Columbus's arrival in 1492, which makes strolling around its fascinating old streets and exploring its rich colonial heritage a real pleasure. The only issue is whether the Dominican Republic's population and its natural environment will be able to withstand the onslaught of mass tourism in the future, limit its potentially destructive side and retain the harmonious atmosphere between locals and visitors.

5

Flower market in Santo Domingo

Position and landscape

Hispaniola is the second-largest island after Cuba in the Greater Antilles, the collective name for the part of the Caribbean island chain which was formed after the North and South American continental plates drifted apart around 140 million years ago. The island has an overall surface area of approximately 76,500sq km (29,500sq miles), 48,500sq km (18,700 sq miles) of which is taken up by the Dominican Republic on the eastern side. The Republic itself has almost 1,600km (1,000 miles) of coastline, and is bordered to the north by the Atlantic Ocean, to the south by the Caribbean, and to the east by the 8,500-m (27,886-ft) deep Mona Passage.

The landscape of the Dominican Republic is especially magnificent. The mountain ranges and hills on the island run northwest-southeast, with lush green valleys between them. The mountains of the Cordillera Septentrional, or Northern Highlands, extend across the coastal zone between Puerto Plata and Nagua, with their foothills extending as far as the Samaná Peninsula. Here the fertile Cibao Valley connects with two large rivers, the Río Yaque del Norte and the Río Yuna. The valley extends over 200km (120 miles), from Monte Cristi as far as Sánchez.

The center of the island is dominated by the Cordillera Central, or Central Highlands, which reaches 3,175m (10,417ft) at Duarte Peak, the highest point in the West Indies. To the southwest are the San Juan Valley, the Sierra de Neiba, the Enriquillo Basin (44m/144ft *below* sea-level and thus the lowest point in the West Indies) and the Sierra de Baoruco. In the southeast, the plain of Santo Domingo extends along the coast from the capital to Punta Cana. It is bordered farther inland by the Cordillera Oriental, or Eastern Highlands. Two important rivers have their source here: the Río Ozama and the Río Chavón.

The Cordillera Central

Climate and when to go

Since the island of Hispaniola lies on the edge of a tropical zone, the climate is generally warm and humid (70–90 percent humidity), and alternates between a rainy season in summer and a dry season in winter. Statistically speaking, the months with the most rainfall are May and August; the least rain falls in January and February. The precipitation affects the various regions in different ways. Since the weather is significantly influenced by the northeastern and southeastern trade winds, the eastern slopes of the Cordillera get quite a bit of rain, as do the Samaná Peninsula, the north coast, the region around San Cristóbal and the eastern slopes of the Sierra de Baoruco. Extremely dry regions sheltered from the winds include the region around Monte Cristi, the Enriquillo Basin and the southeastern part of the Republic, east of Higüey. The showers, although heavy, are usually very short, and bright sunshine usually returns within a few hours.

As far as climate is concerned, there is no ideal time of year to visit the Dominican Republic because the weather is superb the whole year round. The July to November period does, however, bring the odd hurricane. Daytime temperatures along the coast fluctuate between 80°F (27°C) and 90°F (32°C) all year long, and at night it hardly ever gets any colder than 68°F (20°C). The mountain regions are of course cooler; high in the Cordillera in January, temperatures can often fall below freezing point. Water temperatures fluctuate between 78°F (26°C) and 88°F (31°C).

Laguna Gri Gri and Juan Dolio

Politics and administration

The Dominican Republic is composed of 29 provinces and the municipal district of Santo Domingo. The constitution of the Republic's representative democracy, promulgated in 1966, vests executive power in the president who is directly elected to a four-year term. Having occupied the post at the end of the dictator Trujillo's era and again from 1966 to 1978, Dr Joaquin Balaguer managed a further three consecutive terms from 1986 until 1996, when he was replaced by Dr Leonel Fernández Reyna. The constitution has been amended 29 times since it was first drawn up in 1844, and it places the president in a relatively strong position: he is commander-in-chief of the armed forces and also chief of police. Legislative power is vested in the bicameral Congress, comprising the Senate (30 members) and the Chamber of Deputies (130 members). Since 1994 the voters have had four votes each: for the president, the members of the Chamber of Deputies, the members of the Senate, and the members of the district councils. The president also needs an absolute majority and may not be re-elected twice in a row.

Numerous parties were formed during the period following the Trujillo dictatorship (1930–61), and at the moment there are three principal ones. The *Partido Reformista Social-Cristiano* (PRSC), run by ex-president Balaguer, is conservative. The social-democratic *Partido Revolucionario Dominicano* (PRD), founded in exile by Juan Bosch in 1939, was at the helm for six months in 1962 and again from 1978 to 1986. Recently the party has lost much support from the middle classes and from the urban working population, mainly because it introduced reforms only tentatively and was also discredited by several corruption scandals within its own ranks. The party of President Leonel Fernández, the *Partido de la Liberacion Dominicana* (PLD), was created in 1974 by Juan Bosch after he fell out with the PRD; before its election success in 1996, it had attracted support primarily from intellectuals, workers and the poor. The PLD is in favor of cutting ties with the US and also supports a more just distribution of income.

Democracy in the Dominican Republic began in 1961, after the fall of the Trujillo regime, but the various parties, unions and political associations are not the sole source of power. The army, the Catholic church and the financial elite also exercise considerable influence whenever conflicts have to be settled.

The economy

Tourism, the industries of the free trade zones (*zonas francas*) and agriculture are the main sources of revenue in the Dominican Republic, and the most important single cus-

Dominican Republic – a rich mosaic

Balaguer was replaced in 1996

tomer is the US. Free trade zone products, in particular textiles, account for 79 percent of exports and have replaced ferronickel and sugar as the chief export items. A drop in world demand for sugar caused prices to tumble at the beginning of the 1980s, and was combined with other factors such as the increase in the price of crude oil. The economic situation has been improving since 1996, but the state is still deep in debt. After the sugar slump, the government decided to subsidize other exportable commodities; these included coffee, cocoa, tobacco and tropical fruit. Around 40 percent of the total surface area of the Dominican Republic is in permanent agricultural use, and roughly half of it is owned by a handful of powerful landowners and by the state, which confiscated all Trujillo's real estate following the dictator's death.

Fruit is an important commodity

Christopher Columbus came here in search of gold and silver ore, and it's still there, though the upper levels of the government-owned mine near Cotui have been worked out and the costs of digging deeper are prohibitive. Other mineral resources include ferronickel, bauxite, gypsum, iron ore, platinum and rock-salt. As a measure to reduce unemployment the government has introduced free-trade zones where local and foreign firms can set up operations.

Tourism has developed into one of the main sources of income over the past two decades. Between 1987 and 1993 the number of hotel rooms more than doubled, and annual tourist arrivals are now over 2 million. Many hotels and firms are foreign-owned, however, so much of the income is never seen by the ordinary population.

8

Tourism has more than doubled

The environment

Between its arid deserts and high mountains, the Dominican Republic has seven different vegetation levels and thus offers more variety than any other Caribbean island. Thousands of plant and animal species can be found here, none of which – apart from the alligator – is dangerous to man. There again, mosquito bites can be unpleasant, and touching the giant millipedes *(milpiés)* which often live in houses can be very painful. The small geckos scuttling around everywhere provide excellent protection against insects, however.

Heliconia

Along the coast, the coral reefs are home to an astonishing variety of different species of fish, algae and crustaceans. The reefs, which are being threatened by thoughtless coral-collectors, also protect the bays from unwelcome intruders: sharks. The odd accident does get reported, and because of this it's best not to swim in the more remote bays, especially where the water is deep. During the winter months, a fascinating spectacle can be observed north of the Samaná Peninsula: it's the mating season of the humpback whale.

An alligator waits

Protected sections of the coastline contain mangrove forests. The red mangroves are insensitive to salt water and have aerial roots; they can thus survive even when the water level is very high. Black mangroves can be found in more shallow waters. Their roots are home to shrimps, small fish and shellfish, and because of this whole flocks of birds nest in their branches: pelicans, herons, oyster catchers and frigate birds are the most common. Alligators are found near the mouths of the Yaque rivers and in the Enriquillo Basin. Turtles retreat to the more isolated beaches and river deltas to lay their eggs.

The coconut palms provide nourishment but also have a variety of other uses including domestic implements and building construction. The palm forests contain numerous species of birds such as the palm thrush, the *cotica* (the Dominican Republic's national bird, a kind of small green parrot), and the Haitian parakeet.

In the island's interior, the handful of lakes are home to colonies of flamingoes and iguanas. The dry areas in the southwest contain several species of snakes and scorpions; their bites and stings are not life-threatening, but it's best to avoid the areas of dry bush and cactus they tend to inhabit. Wherever more rain falls, dense evergreen forest can be found, containing several exotic hardwoods such as mahogany, and also many rare species of rodents including the opossum shrew, or solenodon.

A large section of the interior is planted with monocultures, especially bananas and sugar cane. Cabbage palms and the majestic 30-m (100-ft) high royal palm can often be seen growing on these plantations. Areas that have so far been left untouched by agriculture contain large quantities of hibiscus, oleander, azalea and philodendron – all of them familiar as house plants in Europe – and the magnificent flame tree. The island also has more than 60 different kinds of orchids, with nearly 300 sub-species.

9

Palm-lined beaches

Iguanas need protecting

To protect the threatened flora and fauna and also to preserve the island's trees, nature reserves were created in the Dominican Republic during the 1970s. Today around 11 percent of the country is protected by eight national parks and several smaller reserves. Growing tourism is presenting problems, however, and for this reason only a few select companies offering excursions are allowed inside the park areas. The state-run firm of Ecoturisa, for instance, operates cultural and scientific trips through regions of ecological interest. Travelers wishing to explore the parks and reserves on their own should apply for a permit from the National Parks Administration in Santo Domingo (*see pages 81 and 86*).

Population

There are more young than old people

The Dominican Republic has a population of some 8.2 million, approximately one-third of whom live in the urban areas. As in most Third World countries there are more young than old people. Thirty-eight percent are below the age of 15, while only 5 percent are older than 60. Eleven percent of Dominicans are black, 16 percent are white, and 73 percent are *mulatto*, i.e. of mixed European and African ancestry. Mulattos often refer to themselves as 'white' or 'dark Indians' *(indio claro, indio oscuro)*, even though the few Indians who lived on the island were almost completely exterminated by the Spanish a few decades after the arrival of Columbus. This strange custom reveals an underlying identity problem in the Dominican Republic: even though racial equality is firmly upheld, hardly anyone wants to be thought of as being descended from black African slaves, let alone from anyone in highly impoverished Haiti next door where the black population is more than 60 percent. Racial tensions in Dominican everyday life are rare, however, even though social status and skin color do seem to go hand-in-hand: most of the top positions are in white hands. Spanish is the official language.

About two-thirds of the population of the Dominican Republic live on the poverty level. This group comprises the unemployed (30 percent) and the 'under-employed', i.e. seasonal workers, street traders and tour guides, who make up another 25 percent. This social group includes maidservants, too, and smallholders; the latter are migrating to the towns in ever greater numbers, in search of higher incomes.

The relatively small middle class is finding it increasingly difficult to maintain its standard of living. The monthly wage of a teacher in a state school amounts to almost as much as the price of a night's stay in one of the better hotels. Many middle-class people are thus attempting to compensate for the rise in the cost of living by doing jobs on the side. The prosperous upper classes –

Schooling is compulsory

mostly landowners, industrialists and merchants – account for just 5 percent of the total population.

Education

Six years of basic schooling are compulsory in the Dominican Republic. These are followed by four years of higher education which can be extended by two more years of practical training for a profession. Nevertheless, at around 20 percent, the illiteracy rate is relatively high, a situation which the present government is trying to improve by building new schools – particularly in rural areas. Church-funded and private schools have a better reputation than state schools, though the high fees they charge make them a privilege of the few. Among the universities and polytechnics, the Universidad Autónoma de Santo Domingo claims to be the oldest university of the Americas.

A proud principal

Unloved neighbors: the Haitians

You can sometimes see them on the country roads in the evening: shabbily-dressed blacks carrying machetes. They've just earned the equivalent of two or three US dollars for a 12-hour day in the sugar cane plantations, and are now on their way back to the *bateyes*, their dismal lodgings without drinking water or electricity. For decades the Dominican Republic has both officially and unofficially been trying to attract labor for the *zafra*, or sugar harvest, from its bitterly poor neighbor, Haiti – for despite chronic unemployment, it's very rare for a Dominican to cut sugar cane. Many of the Haitian seasonal workers remain in the country afterwards.

As conditions have worsened in Haiti, the number of illegal immigrants to the Dominican Republic has increased; today between half a million to a million Haitians are estimated to be living here. They number among the very poorest in the population, doing jobs the Dominicans consider either too dirty or too demeaning: cutting sugar cane, building roads or acting as messengers.

The Dominicans' attitude to the immigrants is ambivalent: on the one hand they need the labor, but on the other they're tempted to seal themselves off from Haiti completely. There are historical reasons for this: in the 19th century Haitian troops overran the rest of the island on several occasions, and both halves of Hispaniola were ruled for 20 years by the Haitian president, Jean Pierre Boyer. Fear of infiltration survived into the 20th century: in 1937 the Dominican dictator, Trujillo, had 30,000 Haitians hacked to death in the border region. Whenever there is social unrest in the Republic, the old fears are re-awakened and thousands of immigrants are sent back across the border.

Voodoo

Voodoo is practised alongside several Catholic rites in the Dominican Republic, particularly in the more rural areas. In Haiti it is the main religion, and is often celebrated in ecstatic rites. In the Dominican Republic, however, voodoo masses are a lot quieter. People meet at the house of a medium, also known as a *servidor* (servant), in front of an altar covered with pictures of saints, herbs or pearls. As he dances to the sound of drums the medium enters a trance-like state and asks the *seres* for help. These are partly African and partly Indian deities who can also be embodied in Christian saints. Possessed by the spirit, the medium makes prognostications or heals the sick with mysterious magic rituals. He is then showered with presents. After the ceremony there's usually a large feast.

Although it all sounds harmless enough, voodoo has resulted in serious bloodshed. At the beginning of this century the faith healer Olivario Mateo (also known as *Santo Liberio*) lived in the town of Las Martas de Farfán, near San Juan de la Maguana. His religion – a mixture of voodoo and Christianity – won him thousands of followers. He and many others were massacred in 1922, during a showdown with US troops.

In the 1960s the cult underwent a revival in Palma Sola (near Las Matas) when León and Delanoy Ventura, two Liberio priests, collected a large band of followers. Again, the fanaticism ended in bloodshed: on 28 December 1962 the priests and hundreds of their supporters were hacked to death by army troops.

Taíno petroglyph

The Taínos

Until the decade in which their fortunes were to change radically for the worse, the *Taíno* Indians had lived for 1,500 years in their little huts on the island they knew as

Aíti. Members of the same linguistic group as the Arawak Indians, they had arrived on the island from the northern part of South America. In doing so they gradually forced out the Ciboneys, a tribe of hunters and gatherers. The Taínos still fought the odd battle with the warlike Caribs, but they were generally a peaceful people living off agriculture and fishing. Tobacco was used ceremonially, and the Taínos also had a favorite game whereby a rubber ball had to be struck with the buttocks and hips, with the aim of keeping it in the air as long as possible. The Taíno tribe revered its ancestors, and priests were the most senior members of the community. Spirits lived at various locations across the island, marked by wooden and stone statues.

Showcase of Indian Life, Museo de l'Hombre Dominicano

It was in the fateful year of 1492 that three Spanish ships, the *Niña*, *Pinta* and *Santa Maria*, with Christian crosses on their sails, appeared on the horizon. Christopher Columbus had been commissioned by the Spanish crown to seek the sea passage to India. His men, a motley assortment of adventurers, had one ambition in common: to get very rich as quickly as possible. Columbus's ships reached the north coast of the island on 6 December 1492, and on Christmas Day his men built the first Spanish settlement of the New World, La Navidad, near Cape Haiti. When Columbus returned on his second journey at the beginning of 1494 he found the settlement destroyed. All the inhabitants had been murdered, or had died of disease. Columbus then founded La Nueva Isabela, 100km (60 miles) further east.

Columbus the vanquisher

13

The Spaniards made several expeditions into the island's interior in search of gold, robbing the Taínos of their treasures and setting them to work in mines. In 1503 the *encomienda* system was introduced whereby each Spanish settler was allowed to cultivate a piece of land for the Spanish crown; the Taínos were promptly put to work. The Indians did not survive this sudden change in living conditions; many died from diseases imported by the Spanish, others took their own lives, or died at the hands of the gold-crazed *Conquistadores*. Some Taínos dared to resist the Spanish onslaught. The longest battle was waged by Guarocuya, baptized Enriquillo by the Spanish. For 14 years he fought his colonial lords until he managed to get a peace treaty signed between Spain and America in 1533. Today, Dominicans honor Enriquillo as a freedom-fighter; his fight was in vain, however. Of the 300,000 or so Taínos (some put the figure as high as one million) who inhabited the island in 1492, only around 500 were still alive just 40 years later. At the suggestion of Bartolomé de las Casas, a Dominican priest, the Spanish decided to import slaves from Africa. Around 30,000 were transported from West Africa to Hispaniola.

Historical Highlights

ca AD200 The *Ciboneys* are driven off the island by the *Taínos* (*see page 12*).

6 December 1492 Christopher Columbus arrives on the island and names it La Isla Española. The first settlements he builds in the north are destroyed by native Indians.

1496 The town of La Nueva Isabela is built on the south coast, on the eastern bank of the Río Ozama. The settlement, which is built of wood, is destroyed by a hurricane in 1502. A new town, Santo Domingo, is built on the Ozama's western bank.

From 1509 Under Columbus's eldest son Diego Colón, Santo Domingo flourishes as the first Spanish town in the New World. In the 1620s large quantities of gold and silver are also discovered in Mexico and Peru, and the colony gradually loses its former importance. Many of the settlers leave.

1586 Sir Francis Drake, the English explorer and buccaneer, pillages Santo Domingo and razes parts of it to the ground.

1605–6 On orders of the Spanish crown, governor Antonio de Osorio has the inhabitants in the relatively impenetrable north and west of the island resettled in the southern part in an attempt to stop smuggling. The settlements in the north are destroyed. The no-man's-land that remains is settled by the French and by pirates of various nationalities.

1697 Under the terms of the Treaty of Rijswijk, Spain formally cedes the western third of the island to France. The French colony of Sainte-Domingue grows extremely prosperous from the boom in sugar cane, which is based on black slavery, while the eastern part of the island becomes increasingly impoverished. By the mid-18th century, the number of Spaniards in the eastern part of the island has reached barely 2,000 (out of a total of 6,000).

1795 Spain is forced to surrender the eastern part of Hispaniola to France. Meanwhile, in the western part of the island, slave uprisings are growing increasingly common.

1801–4 Fired with the fervor of their rebellion at the turn of the 19th century, followers of Toussaint L'Ouverture and Jean J Dessalines plunder the eastern part of the island.

1804 Dessalines proclaims the independence of the French colony of Sainte-Domingue; the first black republic in America calls itself Haiti.

1809 The eastern two-thirds of the island are returned to Spain.

1821–22 Following the lead of the countries on the mainland, the colony declares its independence as the Dominican Republic, but is almost immediately overrun by the troops of Haitian president Jean-Pierre Boyer.

1838 During the Haitian occupation, the writer Juan Pablo Duarte, the soldier Ramón Mella and the lawyer Francisco del Rosario Sanchez found the secret society known as La Trinitaria (*see page 31–2*).

27 February 1844 Supporters of the Trinitaria, led by Mella and Sánchez, occupy the fortress of Santo Domingo and declare independence. This day is henceforth regarded as marking the foundation of the Dominican Republic.

1861 The controversial president, General Santana, who sent the Trinitaria independence fighters into exile, places the Dominican Republic under Spanish protection again – against the will of the inhabitants.

1863–5 Civil War (War of Restoration) breaks out and ends with the withdrawal of the Spanish and re-establishment of independence.

1880–2 The country is headed by a Roman Catholic archbishop, Archbishop Meriño.

1882 Ulises Heureaux becomes president. Except for a three-year interlude between 1884 and 1887, he presides over a period of unprecedented stability and national growth, but borrows millions of US dollars in the process.

1899 President Heureaux is assassinated, leaving the country deep in debt.

1916–24 Having managed the country's customs affairs (on behalf of US and foreign creditors) since 1905, the United States occupies the Dominican Republic in accordance with the Monroe Doctrine. During the occupation, new roads, schools and communications facilities are built; the Americans also secure a large share of the island's raw materials and mineral resources.

1930–61 The dictator, Rafael Leonidas Trujillo y Molina, comes to power and remains in control for three decades. During that time the Trujillo clan grows extremely rich. Corruption flourishes and political opponents are tortured.

1937 An estimated 10,000 Haitian immigrants are slaughtered, prolonging the hatred between the two republics.

1961 Trujillo is assassinated on 30 May; his puppet president at that time is Joaquín Balaguer, who sets about eradicating his family's influence.

1962 Juan Bosch, leader of the Partido Revolucianario Dominicano (PRD), wins the first democratic presidential elections. Seven months later he is forced to leave office following a military putsch led by Colonel Elias Wessin y Wessin, and goes into exile.

1963 A military 'triumvirate' assumes power and appoints the civilian, Donald Reid Cabral, as president. This conservative government meets with massive popular resistance.

1965 With the help of a group of young colonels, the 'Constitutionalists', supporters of Juan Bosch, take control of Santo Domingo. Fearing a second Cuba, US President Lyndon Johnson sees no alternative but to intervene militarily.

1966 Trujillo puppet Joaquín Balaguer at the head of the Partido Reformista Social Cristiano (PRSC) wins the presidential elections. Balaguer promotes foreign investment, wage freezes and an increase in exports; in foreign policy he follows a strictly pro-American line.

1978 The social democratic PRD wins the elections under Antonio Guzmán. Guzmán commits suicide in 1982 after discovering that members of his family have been involved in corruption, but the party remains in power until 1986.

1986, 1990, 1994 The ageing Balaguer is elected president three more times, on the last occasion only narrowly defeating his rival.

1991 Balaguer orders the deportation of all illegal Haitian immigrants under the age of 16 and over 60. Negotiation of accord with the IMF leads to demonstrations and strikes.

1992 The Republic makes expensive preparations to celebrate the 500th anniversary of Columbus's arrival on Hispaniola, in the face of several protests at the 'glorification of colonialization'.

1996 Presidential elections won by Leonel Fernández Reyna of the PLD.

1998 Hurricane Georges devastates parts of the country, notably the Sabana Perdida shanty town where 200 people are killed. Damage exceeds US$1.2 billion and thousands are left homeless. Only 5 percent of the tourism centers are hit.

1999 Joaquín Balaguer declares his intention to stand in the 2000 presidential elections.

The Riddle of Columbus's Tomb

On 20 May 1506, almost two years after his final visit to the West Indies, Christopher Columbus died in Valladolid in Spain. Three centuries later his (alleged) last request was fulfilled: his remains were transferred to the cathedral in Santo Domingo for interment. When Spain was forced to cede Hispaniola to France in 1795, one of the coffins in the Columbus vault was hastily taken to Havana. It remained there until Cuban independence in 1898 when the Spaniards wanted Columbus brought back to Spain; he was shifted to the cathedral in Seville.

Dominicans don't agree with this version, however: they are convinced there was a mix-up when the coffin was removed in 1795. Apparently, Christopher Columbus's coffin was left behind, and it was the coffin of his son, Luis Colón, which eventually found its way to Seville. During renovation work on the cathedral in Santo Domingo on 10 September 1877, a coffin was discovered bearing an inscription that clearly referred to Christopher Columbus. In 1898 Columbus was provided with a marble-and-bronze mausoleum in the Basilica Menor, and since 6 October 1992 people can feel close to the *Gran Almirante* ('great admiral') in the Faro a Colón.

The Malecón promenade
Preceding pages: Cabarete beach

Route 1

Santo Domingo

The Oldest Town in the New World

No visitor to the Dominican Republic should miss Santo Domingo; its cosmopolitan flair forms a delightful contrast to other, more provincial parts of the country. A visit to the capital also provides a complete picture of the island and its people. The sights here – especially the architecture – cannot be found in such a high concentration anywhere else on Hispaniola. It's best to reserve two days for this trip, in order to get to know the Zona Colonial, or old town center. After that, there's more to explore beyond the town walls in the 'Western New Town', and also in the east on the other side of the Río Ozama.

The Panteón Nacional

Santo Domingo covers an area of 162sq km (62sq miles). It has several universities, an international airport and is the industrial center of the country. An increasing number of people are moving here from the rural areas, hoping to find work and a modest income. The fast-growing city has long since spread beyond its natural borders: the Río Haina to the west, the Río Ozama to the east and the Río Isabela to the south. The city's expansion is causing severe social problems. The gulf between rich and poor can be traced on the map. The villas of the wealthy are located in the northern suburbs. The city center and the formerly prosperous residential area known as Gazcue are shared today by the middle classes; and the poorer sections of the community have been forced out to the edges. There are slums to the north along the banks of the Río Ozama, and along the main streets leading out of the city.

El Conde pedestrian precinct

History

In 1496, Christopher Columbus' brother, Bartolomé Colón, founded the settlement of *La Nueva Isabela* on the eastern bank of the Río Ozama. The wooden buildings were destroyed by a hurricane shortly afterwards, and in 1502 the settlement was moved across the river and re-named Santo Domingo. Over the next few decades it flourished, becoming the seat of a viceroy and a bishop. When gold was discovered in Mexico and Peru in the 1620s, however, many Spaniards emigrated to the mainland.

Sir Francis Drake's attack in 1586 almost finished off Santo Domingo; his men pillaged the town and burned large areas to the ground. Until the 19th century the town became increasingly less important, and was also severely damaged by a series of earthquakes. Its fortunes revived somewhat briefly after the Dominican Republic was founded in 1844, but it was under the dictator Trujillo, when Santo Domingo was re-christened 'Ciudad Trujillo', that construction work really began again in earnest. From 1930 onwards new suburbs were built to the west of the old town, and the large *avenidas* and the Malecón (harbor promenade) were laid out. In 1961 the city had a population of 400,000 and covered a surface area of 62sq km (24sq miles). When President Balaguer came to power in 1966, more construction work began in the east.

By 1981 Santo Domingo had 1.4 million inhabitants, by 1990 1.8 million, and now the figure is almost 3 million. The daily power cuts, the water supply problems and the polluted rivers illustrate the immense task facing the politicians in the coming years.

19

Zona Colonial

It was on the west bank of the Río Ozama, at the point where the river flows into the Caribbean, that the chess-board-like center of today's Santo Domingo was built in the first decades of the 16th century. In those days the Zona Colonial was the main Spanish base for forays into the American continent, and the magnificent religious and secular structures, many of which can justly be said to have been 'the first of their kind in the New World', date from this period. The ensuing centuries of stagnation here did have one positive result: the early colonial architecture is still largely intact. Even though the buildings suffered from pirate raids, invasions and natural catastrophes, they were never torn down and built over like their counterparts in the more prosperous colonial cities.

In 1964 a group of architects decided on a restoration plan, and President Balaguer made available the necessary funds. A second, larger wave of restoration began at the end of the 1980s when the Republic started its preparations for the 500th anniversary of Columbus's arrival.

Casa de Bastida and the ruins of San Nicolás de Bari hospital

City Tour 1: Zona Colonial (eastern part)

This trip through the eastern part of the Zona Colonial contains numerous architectural firsts in a very small area: it begins with the first ever cathedral in America, leads along the first ever cobbled street, the Calle Las Damas, to the seat of the Spanish court, the Alcázar de Colón, and ends in the Calle Hostos beside what remains of the first hospital. For quick walkers, the tour can be done in a day; more time is needed, however, if the collections in the Museo de las Casas Reales or in the Alcázar are to be properly appreciated.

Columbus Memorial

Begin the tour at the **Parque Colón** with the bronze-and-granite Columbus Memorial at its center, erected in 1887 during the dictatorship of Ulises Heureaux (1885–9). The four ships' hulls at the corners of the base symbolize the four voyages of Christopher Columbus. The southern side of the square is dominated by the ★★ **Basilica Menor** ❶. In 1521 the first bishop, an Italian named Geraldini, laid the foundation-stone for this cathedral after he had written a letter to Emperor Charles V complaining that 'as a bishop he had no roof over his head'. The majestic structure was

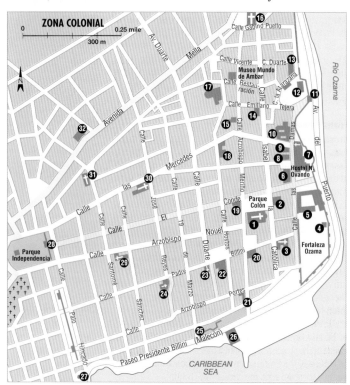

completed in 1540, and in 1546 Pope Paul III raised it to the status of Cathedral of the New World. During the battles for the new colonial territories the building was used by Sir Francis Drake as a barracks. In 1877, in the course of renovations, a tomb was discovered which many believed was that of Christopher Columbus (*see page 15*); a number of archbishops and presidents also lie buried here. Simon Bolivar, an ancestor of the famous South American freedom fighter, is interred beneath the nave.

The cathedral is a three-aisled Late-Gothic structure with a raised nave. It occupies an area of 3,000sq m (3,585sq yds) and is 54m (177ft) long, 23m (75ft) wide and 16m (52ft) high. The pressure of the vault is lessened by mighty flying buttresses clearly visible from outside. Over the centuries 14 chapels have been built.

The western facade is the most attractive. Ornate Plateresque sculpture adorns the twin-arched porch, and the surfaces between the pillars and pilasters are adorned with frescoes of saints. At the end of the southern transept is the Puerta del Perdón, through which the clergy used to pass on the way back to their homes. The cross outside the portal symbolized the right to political asylum for the persecuted. The church is entered today through its northern door. The battlements on the portal are a reminder that the cathedral was once surrounded by a fortified town wall.

Basilica Menor: porch with detail

The graceful interior

The generously-proportioned cathedral interior is impressive, with its round columns leading up to the mighty ribbed vault above. The polygonal presbytery, flooded with light, is most striking. The 14 chapels inside the Basilica Menor were added after the main structure was complete, and are artistically decorated. The Capilla Santa Ana in the southeastern corner contains the tomb of the wealthy Conquistador son and later bishop, Rodrigo de Bastidas (*see page 23*); the Gothic window and Renaissance arch at the entrance to the chapel typify the mixture of styles in the church as a whole. The Capilla de Nuestra Señora de la Luz, on the north side, is where the remains of Christopher Columbus were kept until 1992; the Capilla de los dos Leones, on the west side directly adjacent to the north entrance, contains the tomb of Bishop Geraldini, who built the church and who died in 1524; the monument shows his coat-of-arms above two stone lions, and a wooden crucifix bears an inscription recording the decision to build the church. The elaborate stonework in the Capilla de las Animas, on the left next to the apse, is a masterpiece of the Plateresque style.

Finally, note the Habsburg double-headed eagle in the inside of the western wall. It dates back to Emperor Charles V (1500–50), who ruled an empire 'upon which the sun never set' at the time the church was built.

On the eastern side of the Parque Colón is the striking **Palacio de Borgellá ❷**, built during the Haitian occupation in the first half of the 19th century. The rooms behind the two-story arcaded facade will be accommodating the Dominican 500th Anniversary Committee until 1998. Walk south down the Calle Isabel la Católica. On the corner of Calle Padre Billini is the church of **Santa Clara ❸**, which was built between 1552 and 1556. The interior of this single-aisled church – originally consecrated to Saint Anne – has a marvelous coffered ceiling and a gilded mahogany altar. The convent next door was the first on the island.

Continue eastwards along the Calle Padre Billini and turn left at the next corner. You are now standing in Santo Domingo's first ever street, the **★★ Calle las Damas**, former haunt of Maria de Toledo's ladies-in-waiting (*see page 24*). Many of the city's profane structures can still be admired here.

Fortaleza Ozama

The **Fortaleza Ozama** (9am–4pm, closed Tuesday), at the mouth of the Río Ozama, is the oldest fortified structure in Santo Domingo. Built in the early 16th century, this complex of buildings was given its neoclassical entrance in 1787, during the reign of Charles III. The inner courtyard is dominated by the 20-m (65-ft) high **Torre del Homenaje ❹** ('Tower of Homage'). Rebellious Indians were imprisoned and tortured behind the 2-m (7-ft) thick walls here, and the tower was still in use as a prison during the early days of the Republic. The uprising against Haitian occupation began here in 1844. Until 1924 all the nations that occupied Santo Domingo flew their flags from the top of this tower. To the south of it is a flat 18th-century building with 3-m (11-ft) thick walls – the former arsenal, named after St Barbara, the patron saint of

Palacio de Borgellá   artillery gunners. Between the tower and the arsenal, sec-

tions of ruined wall can be made out on the side facing the river-bank. The water used to reach up to here at one stage, and it was from this location that any enemies arriving by sea would be attacked. The dictator, Trujillo, ordered a higher wall to be built around the Fortaleza area so that the buildings could not be made out from the river. Whether such an investment was sensible in the 20th century is questionable.

Next to the fortifications is the **Casa de Bastidas** ❺ (9am–5pm). This house is named after its first owner, Rodrigo de Bastidas, who was not just one of the most influential men on Hispaniola but also made a name for himself as a colonizer in several other countries of the New World, notably Colombia. His son (*see page 21*) was the bishop of Puerto Rico and of the town of Coro in Venezuela. The sheer size of the arcaded inner courtyard – one of the finest surviving from that time – reflects the importance of the Bastidas family. Today the restored building contains libraries and art collections. Further north along the Calle Las Damas, take a quick look to the left down the El Conde pedestrianized zone; the restaurants put their tables and chairs outside during the evenings so their patrons can dine in the open air with music and candlelight. Just beyond the El Conde is the **Casa de Francia** ❻. The French embassy organizes exhibitions and other cultural events here. The foyer contains a collection of interesting agricultural implements from a Cuban tobacco farm.

The **Hostal Nicolás de Ovando** ❼ was built between 1510 and 1515 by Indians under the supervision of Nicolás de Ovando, governor of the island from 1502 to 1509. Enter the house by the main portal and you will find yourself in the middle one of its three courtyards, which today has a swimming pool at its center. The house was restored in 1978 and turned into a hotel; it's the ideal place to stay for those fond of the colonial atmosphere. Integrated into the hotel complex is another private home from the early colonial era, that of the merchant Francisco Dávila. It even had its own fortifications, the ruins of which can still be seen above the river. The Capilla de los Remedios was once the private chapel of the Dávila House. Its main entrance (usually closed) is on the Calle Las Damas; this is where the colony's inhabitants attended mass before the cathedral was built.

The building directly opposite the Ovando House was built as a Jesuit church between 1714 and 1745. Following the departure of the Jesuits from the island in 1767 the church became a tobacco warehouse and then a theater, before Trujillo had it converted into the **Panteón Nacional** ❽ in the 1950s. Today it contains the mortal remains of the 'immortals of Dominican history'. The bronze can-

Casa de Bastidas

23

Guarding the nation's heroes

The Casas Reales

delabra was a present to Trujillo from the Spanish dictator Franco, and the wrought-iron doors inside the building with their swastika motifs are said by some guides to have come from German concentration camps.

At the corner of the Calle Las Mercedes is the early 16th-century **Casa de los Jesuitas 9**, which was acquired by the Jesuit Order in 1711. Several of the rooms today form part of the Museo de las Casas Reales *(see below)*.

On the opposite side of the street is the mighty facade of a massive complex of buildings, the **Casas Reales 10**. The front section of these 'royal buildings', which were erected in the early part of the 16th century, was taken up by the royal court of justice *(Real Audiencia)* and the audit office; the rear section contained the governors' residence and the island's military administration. The only eye-catching feature on the eastward-facing main facade is the attractive Plateresque window above the entrance.

The Casas Reales had various uses over the centuries until the ★★ **Museo de las Casas Reales** (9am–5pm, closed Monday) moved here at the end of the 1970s. The exhibition is certainly one of the most important in the country and documents economic, political, cultural and military life from the island's discovery and conquest to its independence from Spain in 1821. Two highlights are an almost completely preserved 18th-century pharmacy and a weapons collection with exhibits from all over the world. Opposite the Casas Reales is a small sundial, installed here in 1753 on the orders of governor Francisco Rubio y Peñaranda, and placed slightly at an angle so that the governor and his men could see what time it was from their office windows.

Carry on walking northwards as far as the **Puerta de San Diego 11**, once the most important gate in the city (1578). The eroded remains of three coats-of-arms – those of Santo Domingo, Spain and the island of Hispaniola – can still be seen on its eastern facade.

Alcázar de Colón

The palace complex known as the ★★ **Alcázar de Colón 12** (9am–5pm, closed Tuesday) dates from around 1510, and the central section is lent particular emphasis by the two-story Renaissance arcaded facade, eclipsing the unadorned side sections. More than 1,000 Indians were forced to build this structure, for which apparently not a single nail was needed. The Alcázar was the residence of the first viceroy of the New World, Columbus's son Diego Colón, who was married to Maria de Toledo. Descendants of the Colón family lived in this impressive building until 1577. Many of the works of art and items of furniture (not all of them original) and also the exquisitely decorated wooden ceiling *(bigas)* were presents from the Spanish government.

In front of the Alcázar is the generously-proportioned
Plaza España, appropriately nicknamed the *Plaza del Solazo* ('Sunburn Square') by the locals, because of its lack
of shade. The western side of the square marks the start
of the ★★ **Atarazanas Quarter**. During the 16th century this is where the town's main warehouses were located, and some of the attractively restored houses have
been converted into bars or souvenir stores. The smart
brasserie **Pat'e Palo** and the chic **Museo de Jamón**, where
dozens of hams hang from the ceiling, are popular with
artists, intellectuals and tourists, too. Walk northwards
down the Calle La Atarazana and you'll find several galleries on the left, and the **Bachata Rosa**, where, while sipping your drink, you can enjoy live music performed by
such famous Merengue bands as '4-40'.

Attractive Atarazanas

Highlights inside the **Museo de las Atarazanas Reales**
🔞 (9am–5pm, closed Wednesday) include artefacts salvaged from four ships sunk off the Dominican coast, one
of which was the three-masted *Nuestra Señora de la Concepción*. In 1641 this ship was separated from its Spainbound 'silver fleet' by a severe hurricane, and it struck a
reef. In its hold it was carrying silver which today would
be worth around US$52 million. In 1687 William Phipps,
an Englishman, discovered the wreck and part of the silver, but it was only in the 1970s that the remainder of the
cargo could be salvaged.

25

The 17th-century brick-built Puerta de las Atarazanas
lies on the bank of the Río Ozama; its wedge-shaped front
section, specially designed to ward off intruders, has
earned this gate the nickname *la flecha* ('the arrow'). Beyond it is the **Plaza Arqueología la Ceiba**. Excavations
here have revealed sections of the former harbor. Plaques
provide information on which section of ruined wall belonged to which building. The square is named after the

Girl about town
Parque Arqueología la Ceiba

Casa del Cordón

Casa de la Moneda

Iglesia Santa Bárbara

kapok tree *(ceiba)* to which Christopher Columbus is supposed to have tied his ship when he first arrived.

Walk back through the gate now and along the Calle Vicente Celestino Duarte as far as the Calle Isabel la Católica, then turn left. Juan Pablo Duarte, the founder of the Republic, was born at house No 308 on 26 January 1813. The **Juan Pablo Duarte Museum** here contains several of his personal documents and artefacts.

Two blocks farther on, turn down the Calle Emiliano Tejera. The first house on the left is the ★ **Casa del Cordón** , which according to the inscription is the 'oldest (European-built) stone structure in America'. The building is named after the magnificent stone cord on the portal decoration. It was restored in 1974 and is now a bank. The employees provide a visiting permit on request, allowing access to the rooms and the two inner courtyards. Diego Colón and Maria de Toledo stayed here while the Alcázar was being completed, and Sir Francis Drake also used it for accommodation when he pillaged Santo Domingo in 1586.

Continue westwards along the Calle Emiliano Tejera as far as the next intersection. Then walk about 50 yards down the Calle Arzobispo Meriño to the left, as far as house No 358, the **Casa de la Moneda** ⑮. This building dates from 1542 and is thought to have formed part of a mint. The Plateresque portal is very striking: its central medallion depicts a young man in Renaissance dress, possibly an idealized Charles V, the emperor who accorded the colony the right to mint its own coins.

This is a good place to make a quick detour. Go up the Calle Arzobispo Meriño and soon a small square comes into view. Located here in the former stonemasons' *(canteros)* quarter is the **Iglesia Santa Bárbara** ⑯. Built in 1578 and severely damaged 100 years later, this building has several Mudéjar features alongside its baroque elements. The right of the two unequal towers has a stone window with fertility symbols; the section of facade directly above the entrance is broken up by baroque ornamentation. Inside, the Isabellian-style decoration – small pearl-like rows of stone balls – on the windows and arches is particularly striking. Juan Pablo Duarte, the founder of the Republic, was baptized in this church on 4 February 1813, and his father lies buried here. Behind the church, a flight of steps leads up to the remains of the 18th-century fortress of Santa Bárbara.

Back on the Calle Arzobispo Meriño, at the corner of the Calle Restauración, stands a colonial building housing the **Museo Mundo de Ambar**. Various different types of amber are displayed here, in varying shades from yellow to red and even blue. There are also videos, slide shows and a hands-on corner for children.

A block further to the west the mighty ruin of the **Convento San Francisco** ⓱ comes into view. This 16th-century Franciscan monastery originally consisted of three sections: the large church, the Capilla de la Tercera Orden (Chapel of the Third Order) and the monastery building itself, complete with cloister and cistern. A massive archway leads into what remains of the single-aisled monastery church. The entrance to the convent – a doorway decorated with Franciscan coats-of-arms and cords – has also survived. This is where the Taíno Guarocuya (*see page 13*) was brought up by the monks, and baptized 'Enriquillo'. In 1673 an earthquake severely damaged the monastery complex.

Convento San Francisco

Above the intersection of Calle Hostos and Calle Las Mercedes are the ruins of the **Hospital San Nicolás de Bari** ⓲, the first hospital in the New World. The foundation-stone was laid in 1503 by Governor Nicolás de Ovando, but the basilica-shaped building was only finally completed in 1551. San Nicolás de Bari could accommodate around 60 patients. Although the building was a masterpiece of Spanish colonial architecture and survived several earthquakes, parts of it became so dilapidated that they had to be torn down in 1909. Beside the high outer walls, brick arches, capitals, and foundation walls still survive from various ancilliary buildings.

Hospital San Nicolás de Bari

Continue straight on and turn left on the El Conde, to get back to the Parque Colón. The building with its striking-looking tower on the right-hand corner is the **Old Town Hall** ⓳. It dates from the end of the 16th century, but underwent some radical alterations at the beginning of the 20th century. It's known locally as *El Vivaque* (Bivouac House), because during the Haitian occupation the soldiers used to come here to receive their daily orders. The **Restaurante El Conde** in the square is a cooling place to relax now, after your stroll through the centuries.

27

Parading on the Malecón

City Tour 2: Zona Colonial (western part)

Around half a day should be reserved for this tour, which also begins at the Parque Colón. It leads through the magnificent Callejón Quarter southwest of the cathedral, where priests still live today just as they always have, and along the Malecón, Santo Domingo's harbor promenade, as far as the Parque de la Independencia. After a coffee break you can stroll back through the El Conde pedestrian precinct, making a brief detour to the Mercado Modelo which, like the Avenida Duarte, is very much the center of bustling daily life.

Walk southwards down the Calle Arzobispo Meriño as far as the **Plaza Padre Billini** with its memorial to Father Javier Billini (1837–90), who is reputed to have discovered the urn containing Columbus's remains in the nearby cathedral in 1877. On the southern side of the square is the **Casa de Tostado ⊘**. The writer Francisco de Tostado, who arrived on Hispaniola with Ovando's fleet in 1502, had this house built for himself in 1516. It has an interesting Gothic double window above the main entrance, apparently the only surviving one of its kind in America. The building, which also has a magnificent inner courtyard, today houses the ★ **Museo de la Familia Dominicana** (9am–2pm, closed Monday); here a bedroom, kitchen and living room on two storys depict what living conditions were like for wealthy Dominican families in the 19th century.

Casa de Tostado

A little further up the Calle Arzobispo Meriño on the right is the Casa de Teatro, a house dating from the colonial era which was converted into a small theater and an exhibition center for local artists in 1974. At the end of the street is the **Colegio de Gorjón ⊘**, built by the rich sugar manufacturer Hernando de Gorjón between 1532 and 1537. A school, known as 'Santiago de la Paz y de Gorjón', was founded here by the Jesuits in the 17th century; today the building houses a number of exhibitions.

The Calle Padre Billini opens out westwards into the Plaza Fray de las Casas, at the center of which is a large memorial to the Dominican priest Bartolomé de las Casas (1470–1566), one of the first people to publicly condemn the extermination of the Indians. On the edge of the square stands the **Convento de los Dominicos ㉒**, probably founded in around 1510 and originally a seminary before it became a monastery in 1521. In 1538 Pope Paul III promoted the theological school here to the rank of university (the first in the New World), and it was named 'Universidad de Santo Tomás de Aquino'. It later became the celebrated Universidad Autonóma de Santo Domingo (UASD).

Convento de los Dominicos

The **monastery church** is definitely worth closer inspection. Enter it through the richly-ornamented portal in the west facade, with its fascinating mixture of late Gothic and baroque elements. This church was almost completely destroyed in the 17th century and then rebuilt in the 18th. Of the five chapels, the second on the right is of particular interest: the ★ **Capilla del Rosario**, dating from 1649. Four Roman gods are depicted on the ceiling: Jupiter, representing spring, Mars summer, Mercury fall and Saturn winter. They are accompanied by the 12 signs of the zodiac representing the months of the year. The wooden altar in the apse with its Habsburg double eagle is also very striking. To the right of the Gothic apse, a door leads to the partially preserved cloister. Outside, as you leave the church, the building directly opposite is the 18th-century **Capilla de la Tercera Orden ㉓**, today a community center.

29

Capilla de la Tercera Orden

The palm-shaded **Parque Duarte** is surrounded by a number of well-preserved houses dating from the early part of the 20th century. A memorial stands in honor of the founder of the Dominican Republic, Juan Pablo Duarte (1813–76). A few steps away to the west, on the corner of the Calle José de Reyes, is the former Franciscan church of **Regina Angelorum ㉔**, built between 1550 and 1650. A number of alterations have been made to the building down the years, but some sections, such as the eastern portal, are still original. Inside there are two magnificent baroque altars with silver decoration.

Now walk down the small cobbled lane called **Calle La Regina**. This was where the tailors used to live, and the houses are mostly one story high. Part of the wall of the **Puerta San José ㉕** still survives, and is now decorated with cannon; it can be seen at the intersection of the Calle 19 de Marzo and the Malecón.

Calle La Regina

Monumento a Montesino

On the opposite side of the street is the enormous **Monumento a Montesino** ㉖, depicting the Dominican monk Fray Antón de Montesino shouting his condemnation of the conquistadors' treatment of the Indians across the sea. He denounced the barbaric behavior of the Spanish troops in a famous sermon in 1511, extracts from which can be read on a bronze plaque in the hall beneath the monument. From the second story there's a good view of the old harbor and the promenade, but it's also hard to miss all the rubbish that is thoughtlessly thrown into the sea – a reason why there isn't one acceptable beach in the entire city. The inhabitants have to drive for miles just to find somewhere to swim!

The Malecón

The harbor promenade known as the ★★ **Malecón** extends almost 12km (7½ miles) from the old harbor at the mouth of the Ozama in the east to the western city limits, where it turns into the Carretera Sánchez. The section of it nearest the city center is lined with numerous hotels, cafés, restaurants and discos. In the evenings, during carnival time and at weekends this long promenade is very lively, although the center of the action is gradually moving to the Avenida del Puerto on the west bank of the Ozama. The promenade fills up with flashy cars cruising along to the sound of *merengue* music on the radio.

On the Plaza Rubén Dario is an obelisk known as **La Hembra** ('The Woman') ㉗. The column, shaped like two slightly parted legs, was built to mark the repayment of all foreign debts by Trujillo in 1947. **El Macho** ('The Man'), its counterpart, can be seen 1km further up the Malecón; this phallic column (1937) is meant to commemorate the city's name-change from Santo Domingo to 'Ciudad Trujillo' (*see page 19*). The formerly drab concrete structure has been embellished with colorful paintings of women, the *Hermanas Mirabal*, which the artist Elsa Nuñes sees as symbols of liberty. The ruins of the old San Gil fortifications can be seen below La Hembra.

Leave the Malecón and walk down the Calle Palo Hincado towards the city center. A short distance beyond the remains of the former town wall is the **Puerta de la Misericordia**, where the uprising began in 1844. The Torreón de Santiago and the **Puerta del Conde** ㉘ were also gates in the former colonial wall. The latter's name is derived from Count (*conde*) de Peñalva, who defended Santo Domingo successfully against an English attack in 1655.

Parque de la Independencia

Today the Puerta del Conde functions as an entrance to the **Parque de la Independencia**. At the center of this small park with its canals is the Altar de la Patria, guarded by armed soldiers in full uniform. The marble mausoleum (access only if decently dressed) contains the tombs of the three leaders of the 1844 independence movement: Duarte, Sánchez and Mella (*see page 32*). A bronze wind rose in the park marks the point from which all distances from Santo Domingo are measured; known as *El Kilómetro Zero*, it has developed into a popular rendezvous point. At 5pm every day the flag-hoisting ceremony provides an interesting diversion.

The pedestrianized zone in the ★ **Calle El Conde** is far more modest than magnificent, with its stores selling clothing and shoes, craftwork, hamburgers and ice cream. Apart from the odd turn-of-the-century facade in need of renovation, the street is lined by a series of very ugly concrete structures. However, the stores here contain a many items sought after in vain elsewhere on the island: video and photographic equipment, electrical goods, special books and stationery. The major airlines and banks also have their main offices on El Conde. Here, as everywhere else on the island, anyone who looks vaguely like a tourist is regularly addressed by shoeshine boys, hawkers, moneychangers or cab drivers, all eager to make a deal. The trick is to refuse with a polite smile, unless of course you feel like haggling.

To the right and left of El Conde there are two interesting churches, just a few minutes' walk away. The first is on the corner of Sánchez and Arzobispo Nouel: the **Iglesia del Carmen ㉙**, built in 1729. A small niche above its main entrance contains a delightful Madonna statue just 1m (3ft) high. Inside the church is a famous statue of Christ which is carried through the streets during the procession on Good Friday.

Opposite the little church, on the **Plazoleta de los Trinitarios**, is house No 255; it was here that the *La Trinitaria* secret society (*see also page 14*) was formed in 1838. By that time the country had spent 16 years under Haitian

Chess on the Calle El Conde

31

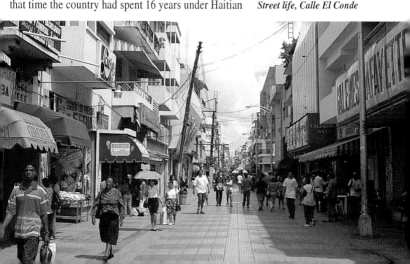
Street life, Calle El Conde

An early stamp of the Republic
Juan Pablo Duarte

domination – ever since the Haitian president, Jean-Pierre Boyer, had sent his troops into the eastern part of Hispaniola and also captured Santo Domingo. The Dominicans were unsure how to respond: some were in favor of an alliance with France, while others such as the landowner Santana wanted the country returned to Spain. A group of young intellectuals had very different ideas, however. They met in secret in 1838, in the Calle Arzobispo Nouel, and laid plans for an independent republic.

The leaders of this secret society, known as *La Trinitaria*, were Juan Pablo Duarte, a law student, Ramón Mella, a young aristocrat, and Francisco de Rosario Sánchez, a black. The secret society worked together with the Haitian underground movement known as *La Réforme*, whose aim was to depose Boyer. The coup succeeded in Haiti in 1843, when Charles Herald became president. In 1844 Santo Domingo was ready for change, too. On 27 February the Haitian-occupied fortress on the Río Ozama was successfully stormed by rebels under the leadership of Mella and Sánchez. Duarte was not with them. He only returned from abroad in 1845, when he was given a hero's welcome as *Padre de la Patria*. The plan was to elect him president, but he refused, thus paving the way for the unscrupulous power-politician Santana, who promptly sent the rebel leaders into exile. During the Civil War *(Guerra de la Restauración)* which broke out in 1863, Sánchez returned to the country; Santana immediately had him executed.

A short distance from the square, on the corner of the Calle Santomé, are the buildings belonging to the **Hospital Padre Billini**. The chapel there, the Capilla San Andrés (1710), contains a very ornate baroque altar with the painting *Cristo de San Andrés*.

North of the El Conde, visit the **Iglesia Conventual de las Mercedes** ③⓪ on the corner of the Calle las Mercedes and the Calle José Reyes. This imposing-looking structure (1527–55) with its massive square tower was once part of a monastery belonging to the Mercedarian Order. The single-aisled church, which contains both Renaissance and baroque elements, can be entered through a side-door in the Calle las Mercedes. Highlights include a bishop's tomb dating from 1644, the fine painting of *Nuestra Señora de las Angustias* (1734), and above all the main altar with its silver decoration which dates from the 18th century. The painting of *Maria de las Mercedes* has also been highly revered ever since it inspired the Spanish poet Tirso de Molina, who lived in the monastery from 1616 to 1618.

Continue a short distance westwards along the Calle Las Mercedes, then uphill along the Calle Santomé to reach the small 17th-century church of **San Lázaro** ③①.

Lepers were looked after here centuries ago; today the complex is a Catholic center. The Gothic chapel and the ornate baroque altar inside can both be visited on request.

The Calle Santomé connects at its northern end with the Avenida Mella. On the right is the modern market building, the **Mercado Modelo** ㉜, entered via a flight of steps. This isn't just a food market, it's also a good place to buy souvenirs and craft products. If you can raise your voice above all the shouting and *merengue* music, it's fun to try and haggle – though the prices here are still higher than in other markets on the island that are off the beaten track and less accustomed to tourists.

The ★ **Avenida Duarte** is where the wealthy shop. People crowd along its narrow sidewalks – made even more cramped by street stalls – to buy all there is to buy. There's one department store after another, and traffic almost always moves at a crawl. This is the very heart of Santo Domingo. At the northern end of the avenue, where it meets the Avenida 27 de Febrero, are the bus and *guagua* (*see page 85*) stops connecting with the east and west of the city.

Mercado Modelo and souvenirs

33

City Tour 3: The West Side

The interesting destinations in the west side of the city are so far from the center that they can hardly be reached on foot. It's best to take a taxi or one of the *Públicos* that travel from the northern side of the Parque de la Independencia westwards, along the Avenida Bolívar. The route back is via the Avenida de la Independencia.

The entrance to the **Parque de la Cultura** is on the Avenida Máximo Goméz. The park was opened in 1966, and contains several museums, a library and a theater. The first building that comes into view is the **Teatro Nacional**,

Teatro Nacional

where operas, ballets and plays are regularly performed; it has a seating capacity of 1,700. Beyond the theater are three museums – allow at least half a day to explore them. The first one is the ★ **Galería del Arte Moderno** (10am–5pm, closed Monday), the only museum on the island to provide a comprehensive view of modern Dominican art; there are also several exhibitions of contemporary work from abroad.

A few steps further on is the **Museo Nacional de la Historia y Geografía** (10am–5pm, closed Monday), which mainly documents recent history, especially the Trujillo era (1930–61); exhibits include weapons, furniture and photographs. On the first floor, three rooms contain items documenting the Haitian invasion and occupation (1822–44, *see page 14*).

Beyond the natural history museum is the ★ **Museo del Hombre Dominicano** (10am–5pm, closed Monday), probably the most interesting of the museums in the park. The history and everyday life of the Indians is illustrated in detail, and juxtaposed with developments after the Spanish conquest. Display cases in the archaeological section show a Taíno village, Indian jewelry and domestic artefacts. The ethnological section is devoted to Spanish and African influences on culture and everyday life; there are several fascinating items of clothing, masks and photographs on display. In the entrance hall of the museum

34

Museo del Hombre:
Taíno sculpture and village life

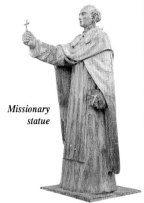

Missionary
statue

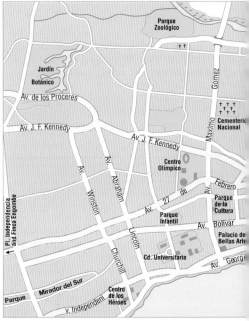

the two white *Papamóviles*, which the pope used on his visits to the island, are displayed.

On the right-hand side of the park is the enormous National Library, and beside it the **Museo de Historia Natural** (10am–5pm, closed Monday). It shows how the island was first formed, and gives a good introduction to its flora and fauna. On the third floor there's a small café with a view of the city and the sea.

The park to the west of the Parque de la Cultura, the **Parque Infantil**, is a good place to take the kids.

There are several cultural sights along the Malecón. East to west, these include the **Palacio de Bellas Artes**, on the corner of Independencia and Máximo Goméz, the second-largest theater in the city after the Teatro Nacional; and also the **Centro de los Héroes**, on the corner of George Washington and Winston Churchill. Trujillo had the enormous Monumento de la Paz (Peace Monument) erected in 1955 to celebrate the 25th anniversary of his rule. After his death, however, the square was turned into a place of commemoration for the 54 Cuban-backed Dominicans who tried to invade the country by plane and topple the dictator in 1959. Photographs of the 54 freedom-fighters can be seen in small individual niches. In the south-western corner of the square is an amphitheater dating from the same period, which has been restored.

Palacio de Bellas Artes

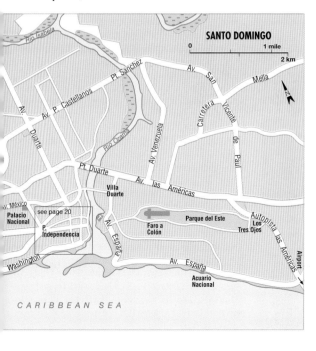

Parque Zoológico railway

Delight in the Jardin Botánico

Palacio Nacional

Northwest of the monument is the **Parque Mirador del Sur**. It extends for more than 7km (4 miles) parallel to the coast, from the Avenida Winston Churchill to the Avenida Luperón in the west. The park, which is intersected by a four-lane highway, was laid out in the 1970s and is a popular place of recreation for hikers, sports enthusiasts and weekend trippers. On Sundays the wide Avenida de la Salud is closed for traffic, to make room for joggers, cyclists and skaters. There are several Indian caves in the park, one of which has been turned into the discotheque 'Guácara Taína'.

The ★★ **Jardin Botánico** (9am–5pm, closed Monday), which was opened in 1976, lies to the north of the Avenida J.F. Kennedy (entrance on Avenida Jardin Botánico) and covers an area of 182 hectares (450 acres). A visit here is a delightful experience, even for those who know nothing about things botanical. A miniature railway takes visitors past palm groves and all kinds of weird and exotic tropical vegetation before arriving at a Japanese garden.

The **Parque Zoológico** (9am–5pm, closed Monday) lies to the north of the city in a former limestone quarry on the banks of the Río Isabela. The main entrance is on the Avenida Zoológico, and a narrow-gauge railway takes visitors across the 160-hectare (400-acre) area with its small lake, children's zoo and alligator pond.

Those with plenty of time on their hands should visit the enormous **Palacio Nacional** (guided tours Monday, Wednesday and Friday), on the intersection of the Avenida 30 de Marzo and the Avenida de México. It was built by Trujillo in 1944 and today is the seat of government. Other worthwhile destinations include the Centro Olímpico (Avenida 27 de Febrero) which has a stadium and various arenas, and the delightful ★ **Orchid Park** (*Orchideario*, Dr José Antonio Polanco) with its 350 different types of orchid.

This tour starts off by taking you to the Villa Duarte quarter on the eastern bank of the Ozama where Christopher Columbus's brother Bartolomé founded the settlement of *La Nueva Isabela*, then to the most monumental and also most recent structure in Santo Domingo, the Faro a Colón, and finally to the Los Tres Ojos caves. Because of the distances involved it's best either to travel by rental car or taxi – and you should allow four to five hours if you want to include the aquarium.

Cross the Río Ozama via the Puente Mella, the southernmost of the three bridges leading to the eastern part of the city (the other two, logically enough, are the Puente Duarte and the Puente Sánchez). Then turn right down the Avenida España; the enormous 'Molinos Dominicanos' grain mill is a good way of getting your bearings. The route to the site of La Nueva Isabela, the first settlement in the south of Hispaniola, leads directly across the factory grounds and through an iron gate.

The **Capilla del Rosario**, which is only of historical interest, has undergone substantial alteration. The chapel was first mentioned in 1544 when the priest, Bartolomé de las Casas, celebrated mass here for a missionary expedition to Guatemala. It reputedly stands on the site where Bartolomé Colón, founder of the city, prayed in an earlier, very provisional chapel made of wood and straw. In the mid-1980s extensive excavations were carried out in this area, and although several interesting finds were made – including artefacts from the chapel and several skeletons – archaeological activity has ceased.

37

Continue southwards now down the Avenida España and turn left into the four-lane Avenida Argentina, which leads directly to the lighthouse memorial known as the ★ **Faro a Colón**. This structure, as controversial as it is monumental, was described by President Balaguer, who commissioned it, as 'the eighth wonder of the world'. The idea of a monument to Columbus is at least a century old. On 24 April 1923 the Fifth Interamerican Conference in Santiago de Chile recommended a project representing 'collective feelings of gratitude, admiration and love for Christopher Columbus, the discoverer of America and benefactor of mankind' – and in 1929 the British architectural student J Cleave won the commission. The 'recumbent cross'-shaped concrete structure, completed in 1992, is based on his original draft. Several slum districts were razed to the ground to make room for it – the monument covers an area of 10,000sq m (11,950sq yds). On the outer walls of the Faro there are plaques bearing the names of the different states of Latin America, and

The Faro a Colón, complete with madonnas

at night (sometimes only at weekends) a cross-shaped laser beam from the center of the cross pans across the sky. A broad flight of steps leads from the west to the center of the monument. Inside, the **marble tomb of Christopher Columbus** is guarded by uniformed sentries; his remains were transferred here from the cathedral (*see page 21*) on 6 October 1992 when the Faro was officially opened. The rooms to the right and left of the long corridor beyond the tomb contain exhibition material covering 50 nations.

The tomb of Columbus

The Faro has been an object of controversy ever since its foundation-stone was laid in 1986; several bombs went off in the Zona Colonial on the day it was opened. The reason is the huge cost of putting on such an extravaganza in a country where half the population lives beneath the poverty level. The laser beams 350,000 watts of power at the heavens above, while the city below has to endure at least one power cut a day and many of its inhabitants have no electricity at all. Nevertheless, President Balaguer defended his lighthouse with the words: 'People need to wear shoes, but they also need to wear a tie. The lighthouse is that tie.'

Beyond the Faro a Colón is the **Parque del Este** with its pinewoods, footpaths and green lawns. At the eastern end of the park, and best reached by car along the Avenida Las Americas, are the caves known as ★ **Los Tres Ojos** ('The Three Eyes', 8am–5pm). The 'eyes' are small sub-terranean lakes located inside this underground cave system, which can be entered via steep flights of steps cut into the rock. After boarding a rope-guided raft and being taken across the second lake and through a limestone cavern you reach a fourth 'eye', another lake, surrounded by lush tropical vegetation. There are rumours that a crocodile has been living here ever since it was left behind by a French film crew. They had brought along three crocodiles from the Lago Enricillo as extras, but one escaped, never to be caught again.

Los Tres Ojos

Those with time on their hands could drive another 2km (1 mile) along the Autopista Las Americas and turn west down the Avenida España at the next major intersection. Along this avenue, beside the sea, is the ★ **Acuario Nacional** (9.30am–6pm, closed Monday), where all manner of underwater fauna and flora can be admired. Turtles, sharks, rays and all kinds of colorful tropical fish swim about in this spacious and well-documented aquarium. One fascinating feature is the glass tunnel, where visitors can walk 'beneath the water' and see the fish from a sea-bed perspective. There are films and lectures on underwater themes in the auditorium every half hour, and a snack with a sea view is a good way to round off any visit here.

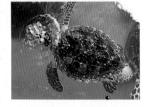

Acuario Nacional

Route 2

Along the Amber Coast

Puerto Plata – Sosúa – Río San Juan – Sánchez – Samaná Peninsula (216km/134 miles) *See map on page 40–1*

The *Costa de Ambar*, or 'Amber Coast', is the name given by Dominicans to their north coast, but it's only half true: the precious resin that flowed out of the pine trees here around 50 million years ago is to be found today several miles inland, in the green hills between Puerto Plata and Santiago. The north coast does hold several other attractions, however, and each year it is visited by an increasing number of tourists from Europe, the US and Canada. Visitors land by plane in the busy holiday center of Puerto Plata, and can travel eastwards to their hotels very quickly along the well-surfaced coast road. Sosúa is experiencing an unprecedented hotel construction boom, and its neighboring resort of Cabarete has become an international windsurfers' paradise; the miles of white sandy beach on the way to Sánchez or along the palm-grove-covered Samaná Peninsula are the perfect backdrop for a genuinely unforgettable Caribbean holiday.

39

Puerto Plata: Parque Central

The tour from Puerto Plata to Samaná and back can be done in two days; anyone interested in taking a boat out from Santa Bárbara in winter to watch the humpback whales mating, or visiting the Los Haïtises National Park should allow themselves more time.

Puerto Plata (pop. 85,000), capital of the province of the same name, is also the largest town on the Atlantic coast. It lies at the foot of the almost 800-m (2,600-ft) high

Puerto Plata and
Pico Isabel de Torres

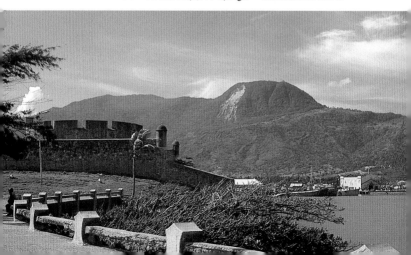

Pico Isabel de Torres (*see page 42*). Puerto Plata was founded in 1502 by Governor Nicolás de Ovando, but later destroyed twice: once at the beginning of the 17th century on the orders of the government in Santo Domingo who considered it a hotbed of smuggling, and resettled the inhabitants of the north to the south; and once again in a serious fire in 1863.

Turn-of-the-century architecture

The attractive houses at the center of the town, with their 'gingerbread'-style wooden decoration on the windows and doors, all date from the turn of the century – which was when Puerto Plata became one of the island's most important harbors. The town was almost completely ignored during the Trujillo era, however, and it was only with the advent of tourism in the 1960s onwards that prosperity gradually returned. Puerto Plata is at its most architecturally charming around the Parque Central. The pretty La Glorieta pavilion at its center was built according to a Belgian design in 1872. The southern side of the square is dominated by the church of San Felipe, constructed just a few decades ago; its matter-of-fact facade is reminiscent of art deco. The grid of streets surrounding the Parque Central – especially the Calle Beller and the western part of the Calle Duarte – contains numerous souvenir stores.

Museo del Ambar Dominicano

At No 61, Calle Duarte, only a few minutes' walk away from the Parque Central, is the privately-run ★ **Museo del Ambar Dominicano** (Amber Museum, 9am–5pm, closed Sunday). On the ground floor several interesting items

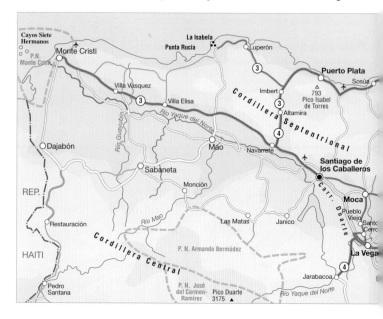

of amber jewelry and other souvenirs can be bought, and on the first floor there is a fascinating exhibition. The principal attraction here is a tiny lizard enclosed in amber; in 1977, an American professor apparently offered US$25,000 for it.

Lizard in amber

At the western end of the harbor promenade, the Avenida Gregorio Luperón, is the **Fortress of San Felipe** de Puerto Plata (9.30am–noon, 2–4.30pm, closed Wednesday; opening times subject to change), the only visible reminder in Puerto Plata of the early colonial era. Built between 1564 and 1577, this bastion was meant to protect the north of the island from raids by pirates and buccaneers. Thanks to restoration work begun in 1973 the almost square fortress now looks very much the way it used to when it was first built: the eastern entrance flanked by two small towers, the massive keep at the center, and the small look-out towers on the two corners of the wall facing the sea. The room on the right as you enter the keep is a military museum; most of the exhibits date from the 18th century. On the left is a small photographic exhibition documenting the restoration work. Both these rooms have very low entrances, so remember to duck. The observation platform on top of the keep is also open to visitors: through the arrow slits you can see the harbor across to the west which the fortress was meant to protect.

San Felipe Fortress

41

Travel westwards, via the Avenida Circumvalación Sur to reach the Carretera 5, and as you leave Puerto Plata the

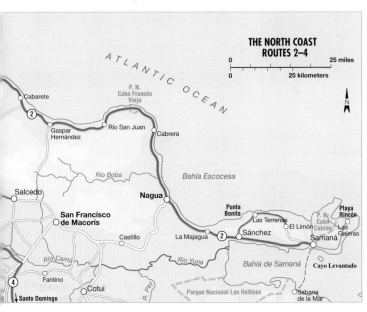

THE NORTH COAST
ROUTES 2–4

0   25 miles
0   25 kilometers

N

ATLANTIC OCEAN

Cabarete
P. N. Cabo Francés Viejo
Gaspar Hernández
Río San Juan
Cabrera
Río Boba
Bahía Escocesa
Salcedo
Nagua
San Francisco de Macorís
Punta Bonita
Las Terrenas
Playa Rincón
P. N. Cabo Cabrón
Las Galeras
Castillo
La Majagua
El Limón
Sánchez
Samaná
Río Camú
Río Yuna
Bahía de Samaná
Cayo Levantado
Fantino
Cotui
R. Payabo
Parque Nacional Los Haïtíses
Sabana de la Mar
Santo Domingo

impressive **★★ Pico Isabel de Torres** (793m/2,600ft) comes into view on the left. A section of rain forest on this mountain is taken up by the Reserva Científica Natural Isabel de Torres, a nature reserve with up to 30 different species of protected birds. Anyone who travels up to the summit will not only have a fantastic panoramic **★★ view** but will also be able to see the 16-m (52-ft) statue of *Cristo Redentor* up close, buy souvenirs, eat lunch or stroll through a botanical garden. There are three ways of reaching the top: on foot, which takes about two hours; by car along a rough road, which takes around 20 minutes; or instead you can take the only cable ropeway *(teleferico)* in the Caribbean (8.30am–4pm, closed Wednesday and Sunday). There's no service on windy days, however, and in peak season be prepared to wait for several hours.

Puerto Plata has some fine beaches. The Long Beach is located at the eastern end of the harbor promenade, and just beyond it are the well-equipped beaches of the Playa Dorada hotel complex, further east is the **Columbus Aquapark**. There are also several small beaches to the west of the town; to find them just follow the 'Costambar' signs. The Playa Cofresí, a pleasant little beach with equally nice hotels, is 7km (4 miles) out of town.

On the beach at Sosúa

The town of **Sosúa** (pop. 11,000), 27km (16 miles) to the east of Puerto Plata, consists of two different sections separated by a half-mile-long sandy beach: the fishing village of Los Charamicos in the west, and the characteristically European quarter known as El Batey to the east of the horseshoe-shaped bay. El Batey owes its existence to the racist policies of two dictators: Adolf Hitler and General Trujillo. Trujillo allowed Jewish refugees to settle here because he thought that an infusion of European blood would 'lighten' the skins of the island's population. At the beginning of the 1940s around 600 Jewish immigrants (rather than the expected 100,000) settled in Sosúa, ploughed the land and very soon developed a flourishing dairy farming industry. Many of those settlers have now emigrated again, but several reminders of their stay survive, including

The synagogue in El Batey

memorial plaques, street-names, a synagogue and also a **Jewish Museum** (in the Calle Dr Alejo Martinez).

El Batey, especially the area around the Calle Pedro Clisante, contains everything a tourist would wish to find: restaurants, cafés, bars, discos, souvenir stores, and also travel firms organising trips. There are several thousand German immigrants living in this area and the place has quite a German flavor to it: there's delicious German bread, and many restaurants serve *schnitzel*. Mass tourism is making distinct inroads, however: the famed hospitality is becoming increasingly money-based, and quite a few young Dominican girls are turning to prostitution.

The road leading eastwards to **Cabarete**, 39km (24 miles) away from Puerto Plata and the Dominican Republic's windsurfing paradise, is lined by dozens of hotels and bungalow complexes. International competitions are held regularly in this small beach resort, which is geared towards the needs of windsurfers of every nationality. Fast-food restaurants, hotels and surfing schools line Cabarete's main street and its mile-long sandy beach.

The well-paved Carretera 5 leads you past miles of palm-lined, deserted sandy beaches, and 90km (55 miles) further on arrives at the fishing town of **Río San Juan** (pop. 10,000). This is a day-trip destination, because nearby is the ★ **Laguna Gri Gri**, at the end of the main street, the Calle Duarte. Boats taking from 10 to 20 passengers set out from a pond-like stretch of water on a two-hour trip along a canal lined with **mangrove trees** which leads to the open sea. The boats circle an area of coral and then chug along the coast, passing several caves, until they enter the largest one, filled with stalagmites and stalactites. A swim in a 'natural pool' *(piscina natural)* is the highlight of the return journey.

Mangroves, Laguna Gri Gri

43

  Almost 20km (12 miles) further along the coast road, a small road branches off to the tiny **Cabo Francés Viejo National Park**, a protected area of rain forest. Right on the coastal road a net stretching over the high rocks indicates the presence of the **Amazonas** animal and bird park. A good place for a break is the **Playa Grande**, visible from the road; the locals living in the wooden huts on the beach make delicious seafood dishes. So lush is the area from Río San Juan around the coast to Cabrera that it is known as the Costa Verde.

Delicious seafood, Playa Grande

  Nagua (pop. 58,000) is 149km (93 miles) from Puerto Plata. Although it is the capital of the province of Maria Trinidad Sánchez, the town has little to offer visitors. On the left as you leave Nagua is the Parque de Recreo with a statue of Maria Trinidad Sánchez, who sewed the first Dominican flag after the victory of 1844. Near Majagua the road veers away from the sea and crosses a flat stretch of land at the foot of the ★★ **Samaná Peninsula**, which was separated from the mainland by a strait until the 18th century, but remains a tropical paradise. Hopefully the Arroyo Barril international airport will not change this.

The quiet town of **Sánchez** (pop. 22,000) was once an important harbor, and also the terminus of the island's only railway line which used to run to La Vega but has now closed. A row of attractive Victorian-style wooden houses still survives from that time. Sánchez is a good place to make a brief detour to ★★ **Las Terrenas** (pop. 13,000) on the north coast of the peninsula. A well-surfaced road,

Las Terrenas beach

rather steep in places, leads off to the left and across a delightful stretch of hilly landscape with luxuriant vegetation; it climbs to an altitude of 450m (1,476ft) before descending to sea-level once more. Las Terrenas is a beach paradise offering absolutely everything: diving, windsurfing, bathing beaches, fish cooked in coconut milk and served right next to the sea, you name it. At the western end of the beach a footpath leads over a small rise to ★**Punta Bonita** (15 minutes' walk) where several beach hotels cater for their guests (to get there by car, turn left as you arrive in Las Terrenas). East from Sánchez, 15km (9 miles) along a badly-surfaced road, is the village of **El Limón**, where a guide can be hired to take visitors on a hike to the 50-m (164-ft) high El Limón waterfall.

After this detour continue east along the Carretera 5 from Sánchez, through a rolling landscape filled with coconut groves and colorful houses. Around 20km (12 miles) from Sánchez a road branches off to Arroyo Barril Airport, and 14km (8 miles) further on is the town of **Santa Bárbara de Samaná** (pop. 40,000), the capital of Samaná Province and usually known as Samaná for short.

Santa Bárbara de Samaná

It was close to this *Golfo de las Flechas* ('bay of arrows'), as Columbus called the bay, that settlers from the Canary Islands founded the community of Santa Bárbara in 1756 at the behest of Governor Rubio y Peñaranda. Numerous freed slaves from the US settled here, too, at the beginning of the 19th century. Their mainly Protestant descendants – named Smith, King or Williams – make up the majority of the rural population. In 1946 there was a serious fire in the town, but the 19th-century Protestant church survived virtually unscathed.

Generally, Samaná, with its broad harbor promenade, is not that idyllic a place. But the beaches in the vicinity are Caribbean paradises, as are the tiny islands in the bay, some of which are connected by footbridges – especially ★ **Cayo Levantado**. Water taxis and fishing boats make

Rare bird in Los Haïtises

regular trips to this island. A good excursion destination by boat from Samaná is the ★★ **Los Haïtises National Park**; highlights here include several species of rare birds, the opossum shrew, and also several limestone caverns containing pre-Columbian wall paintings (*see page 71*).

Another popular pastime off the coast of Samaná in the winter months is ★ humpback whale watching. From December to March, between 2,000 and 3,000 humpback whales come here from the north to mate. Watching them rolling and diving from the boat is a majestic sight; the whales can grow as long as 16m (52ft) and weigh up to 40 tons. The boom in tourism has swelled the fleet of whale-watching boats, however, and some environmentalists are concerned that the animals may be disturbed by all the fuss.

Route 3

On the Trail of Christopher Columbus

Puerto Plata – (Luperón/La Isabela) – Navarrete – Monte Cristi (138km/85 mile)*See map on page 40–1*

The western section of the Amber Coast couldn't be more of a contrast to the eastern one: travelers here are more likely to meet a horse or a mule coming the other way than a car. The arid region around Monte Cristi, close to the Haitian border, has scarcely been touched by international tourism. There's no single coast road, so the sights are often reached along extremely bumpy tracks.

But with the road there now surfaced, visitors will need only an hour to reach the area's principal attraction, namely the ruins of La Isabela, the settlement founded by Columbus more than 500 years ago.

Leave Puerto Plata (*see page 39*) along the Avenida Circunvalación Sur and the Carretera 5 in the direction of Santiago. The detour to **Luperón/La Isabela** begins 20km (12 miles) out of town, and the distance there and back is 88km (54 miles). Near Imbert, just before two large gas stations with snack-stands, the Carretera 30 branches off to the right. The cactus hedges along the side of the road are used to mark real-estate boundaries.

Having traveled 25km (15 miles) along this route and successfully dodged more donkeys and mules than anything motorized, you will see Luperón come into view – a dusty, sleepy fishing village, with little to indicate the presence of the ultra-modern Luperón Beach Resort holiday village 5km (3 miles) away. Turn left off Luperón's long central square in the direction of La Isabela. The jour-

A common form of transport

The remains at La Isabela

Roadside company

Columbus's house

Skeleton with folded arms

ney continues now along a track strewn with rubble, frequented by several herds of animals, for 15km (9 miles) as far as a T-junction, where you turn right. The route continues across a savanna-like landscape for around 4km (2½ miles), running partially parallel to the small Bajabonica river. At the end of it you'll see souvenir stands, a *comedor* (Dominican restaurant) and a fenced-in area of red sand, the **Arqueología Parque Nacional Historico La Isabela** – all that remains of the first ever European settlement in the New World.

When Christopher Columbus returned to Hispaniola on his second voyage (1493–6) he discovered that the settlement of La Navidad (in today's Haiti) had been destroyed and the 39 men he had left behind were all dead – either murdered by Indians or killed by disease. His little fleet made its way eastwards and on 1 January 1494 dropped anchor in a broad, idyllic bay. Here Columbus founded a settlement in honor of the Spanish queen: 'La Isabela'. Begun in the 1950s, excavation work was speeded up in 1992 in preparation for the 500th anniversary. Stone walls today reconstruct the outlines of the main buildings, such as the church (15m/49ft by 5m/16ft) in which the first Mass on American soil was read on 6 January 1494. Some of Columbus's house has now fallen into the sea through erosion; the semicircular tiles in the corner came from the building's first roof. Wooden crosses beyond the church mark the site of the cemetery. Some of the tombs have been excavated; they contain the skeletons of victims of the *Conquista*. The Christian Spanish dead can be recognized by their folded arms. Rebels and prisoners were buried with their hands tied, sometimes facing downwards; the Indians lie in embryonic postures. La Isabela was abandoned in 1498. Finds from the site include iron cannonballs, crucifixes, sections of chain-mail and dagger scabbards.

Near the excavation site is the colonial-style Templo de las Americas memorial church, where the Pope said Mass in 1992 during his visit to the Dominican Republic. The small road to the west of La Isabela which leads either 16km (10 miles) further on to Punta Rucia or back again via Los Hidalgos to the Carretera Duarte is not recommended: it crosses two streams which aren't always passable. It is best to follow the route described back to Imbert.

The trip continues now towards Monte Cristi. After you've crossed the 1,300-m (4,265-ft) Cordillera Septentrional on the Carretera 5, you'll reach a traffic circle 52km (32 miles) further on in the town of Navarrete (marked on some maps as 'José E Bisonó'). The road to the left leads to Santiago, and the right one – the well-surfaced Carretera

1 – to Monte Cristi. From now on the route runs parallel to the Río Yaque del Norte across a broad, fertile plain; the main crops here are rice and tobacco. The barns used for drying the leaves can be seen throughout this region. On the right the peaks of the Cordillera Septentrional are still visible; inland, the foothills of the Cordillera Central gradually come into view.

In the small town of Villa Elisa, a not particularly well-surfaced road leads off to the right to **Punta Rucia** (ca 25km/15 miles), a fishing village at the tip of a promontory, with attractive coastal vegetation and a quiet beach. There are excursions from Punta Rucia to the ruins of La Isabela. Ecoturisa (*see pages 81 and 86*) organises trips to the ★ **Laguna Estero Hondo**. Visitors to the mangrove swamps here are sometimes lucky enough to spot that rarest of Caribbean animals, the manatee.

From Villa Elisa the landscape becomes quite spectacular, mainly because of the lack of rainfall (677mm/26 inches per year). Agaves and cacti, some as high as 3m (10ft), grow in the sandy soil. The last stretch of the trip takes you past the final sandy foothills of the Cordillera Septentrional – and also past several goats who make a habit of wandering into the road.

Monte Cristi (pop. 20,000), capital of the province of the same name, is the last Dominican town in the northwest before the Haitian border. It was founded in 1533 by Juan de Bolaños and 60 other families who arrived here from the Canary Islands. By 1600, like Puerto Plata, it was almost completely deserted, and only began to prosper again in the 18th century. The numerous, ramshackle-looking Victorian buildings bear witness to better days; those were at the turn of the century, when timber and agricultural produce were shipped from Monte Cristi to Europe. The paint is peeling off the courthouse (corner of Avenida

Rice fields on the road to Monte Cristi

Family and other animals

Duarte and Calle Federico Jesus Garcia), and the legal authorities have moved out of this formerly imposing Victorian structure to a new concrete building on the edge of town. Opposite this old courthouse on the left is the small municipal park, the Plaza del Reloj, named after the symbol of the town, a 100-year-old clock that came originally from France.

Drive up the small rise from the Plaza del Reloj and from the camouflaged barracks there's a good view across the very flat landscape surrounding the town. The only distinctive feature is the mountain known as El Morro; its camel-hump shape struck Columbus as strange, too.

The route back out of town leads past several salt-pans and *comedores*. If you continue along the treeless promenade towards El Morro, a small yacht harbor comes into view across to the right; beyond it is a thick mangrove swamp full of small waterways, and across to the left is the small island of Cabrita. The impression of having reached the end of the world is intensified if you follow the stony road up to where it forks: the route off to the left ends in the sea, beyond a small beach framed by weird-looking sandstone rocks. Monte Cristi does have several sandy beaches, including the Playa Juan Bolaño (on the promenade) and the Playa Granja, and the coastal waters here provide some of the best diving on the island, with both wrecks and coral reefs to explore.

It is possible to take boat excursions to the ★ **Parque Nacional Monte Cristi** (530sq km/204sq miles), which also takes in the coastal strip and the group of islands known as Cayos Siete Hermanos. This national park contains several rare birds and reptiles, including alligators. The mangroves' roots are a breeding-ground for many types of fish, and their branches are also a favorite nesting-place for seabirds.

A stalked stork

The predator

48

Route 4

High Mountains and Fertile Valleys

Puerto Plata – Santiago de los Caballeros – La Vega – (Jarabacoa – Constanza) – Bonao – Santo Domingo (240km/149 miles) *See maps on pages 41–2 and 52*

From Puerto Plata this route follows the Carretera 5 southwards for about 52km (32 miles). At the traffic circle just before Navarrete, turn left. The Carretera Duarte continues towards Santiago at some distance from the Río Yaque del Norte.

Around 60km (37 miles) into the journey from Puerto Plata, a forest of traffic signs along the roadside makes it clear that you're approaching an industrial and agricultural center. After a further 10km (6 miles), **Santiago de los Caballeros** (pop. 700,000), the second-largest town on the island, comes into view. Its name is derived from the 30 Spanish nobles *(caballeros)* who founded the town with Columbus's brother Bartolomé in 1495 a few miles northeast of its present-day location while they were searching the interior for gold. After the severe earthquake of 1562 destroyed Santiago Viejo completely, the town was rebuilt on the eastern bank of the Río Yaque. Santiago owes its prosperity first and foremost to rum and tobacco production; many Dominicans claim that the money spent in Santo Domingo is the money that's earned here, in the metropolis of the Cibao Valley.

Santiago: Palacio Consistorial

49

The tour of Santiago begins at the fortress of San Luís, located on a small rise beside the river. In the early part of this century it was used as a prison; today it is a military barracks. There's a fine view of the valley, the bridge leading to San José de las Matas, and the more modern western part of the town from the river promenade, which is appropriately named the Avenida Mirador del Yaque. Turn right about 700m (730yds) further on, down the Calle 30 de Marzo, to reach the Parque Duarte. The south side of the square is dominated by the **Catedral Santiago Apóstol** (1868–95), a mixture of neo-Gothic and neoclassical. The three-aisled church contains a mahogany altar with gold-leaf decoration. Several national and regional figures, including the dictator Ulises Heureaux, lie buried in this church.

Catedral Santiago Apóstol

On the eastern side of the Parque Duarte (corner of Calle 30 de Marzo and Calle 16 de Agosto) is the ★ **Museo del Tabaco** (Tuesday to Friday 9am–noon and 2–5pm; Saturday 9am–noon). Opened in 1984, it is a cleverly-assembled exhibition on the theme of tobacco from the 16th century (when it was first brought to Europe) to the pre-

Centro de Recreo

Cigar factory worker

sent day. Several implements used for tobacco production, processing and transportation can be seen here. Those interested in present-day tobacco manufacture can also visit a real **cigar factory**; it's located 3km (2 miles) out of town on the autopista Duarte, in the direction of Santo Domingo (Tabaccos Don Esteban, tel: 587 9976).

The **Centro de Recreo** is on the western side of the Parque Central. Built in neo-Mudéjar style in 1894, the building is occupied today by a private club; inside, the halls with their carved wooden ceilings bear mute witness to past glory. The adjacent **Palacio Consistorial** dates from the same period and is one of the finest Victorian structures on the island. The Museo de la Villa (Tuesday to Friday 10am–noon, 2–5.30pm, Saturday and Sunday 10am–2pm, closed Monday) inside documents local history.

Just a few steps away from the Palacio Consistorial is the **Centro de la Cultura**, which contains not only a music school and 500-seat theater, but also several exhibition rooms showing works by national and international artists.

Walk from the Parque Duarte past the Gobernación Provincial (provincial government building), northwards up the Calle Benito Monción and left into the Calle Restauración: you'll see a wooden building containing the **Museo Folklórico de Tomás Morel** (no fixed opening times). Inside there are all kinds of fantastic carnival masks and costumes; the carnival in Santiago is particularly famous, and on Sundays in February these masks can be seen in action.

The Calle del Sol, Santiago's busy main shopping street, branches off the northern side of the Parque Duarte. At the intersection with the Calle España is the white-and-green **Mercado Modelo**, which was built in the 1940s. All kinds of crafts can be bought in this two-story building: jewelry, ceramics, wooden figurines and wickerwork. As with all markets, try a bit of haggling.

Market produce

From here it's less than a mile eastwards up the Calle del Sol to the symbol of the town: the **Monumento a los Héroes de la Restauración de la República** (or 'El Monumento' for short). This vast, white marble monument was built by Trujillo in the 1940s to commemorate the heroes who restored the Republic; it is 67m (219ft) high, and contains a museum as well as several works by the now deceased Spanish painter Vela Zanetti. The gigantic column houses an elevator which takes visitors up to the observation platform, with its fantastic panoramic view. Opposite, the new **Teatro Nacional** is modelled on the national theater in the capital, but is somewhat smaller.

Monumento a los Héroes

You can wind up your tour of Santiago with a visit to the **'Bermúdez' rum factory** (9am–noon, 2–4pm, closed weekends) northwest of the town, on the corner of Avenida J Armando Bermúdez and Calle Blanca Mascaro. There are guided tours – and rum tastings.

Located around 21km (13 miles) southeast of Santiago, **Moca** (pop. 50,000), the capital of the province of Espaillat, lies on a mountain slope at the center of coffee and coconut plantations. The town was founded in the 18th century, and its neoclassical church of Nuestra Señora del Rosario next to the small Parque Central has interesting Gothic-style windows. If you follow the rather steep one-way street away from the center towards the intersection for Salcedo and San Francisco de Macorís, to your left you'll see a small **locomotive** on a section of track in the Plaza Viaducto. It's a memorial to the Santiago–La Vega–Sánchez railroad that brought Moca prosperity at the beginning of the century.

51

The locomotive at Moca

Even though Moca has had little to do with the island's history, its inhabitants are still extremely proud of the fact that it was men from Moca who carried out the successful assassination attempt on the dictator, Ulises Heureaux, in 1899.

A well-surfaced road (Carretera 132) leads eastwards from Moca across 12km (7 miles) of delightful landscape filled with banana plants, palm-trees and coconut palms. Like the rest of the Cibao Valley, the area is densely populated; villages of colorfully-painted wooden houses line the road.

Smile from the countryside

A detour off the beaten tourist track to **Salcedo** is highly worthwhile, not only for those interested in architecture but also because of political history. At the entrance to the village is a square with a small modern metal sculpture. Portraits on the wall enclosing the square commemorate the *Tres Hermanas Mirabal*. They were placed here in 1990 for the 30th anniversary of the deaths of the 'three Mirabal sisters', who were murdered on 25 November

1960 by Trujillo's thugs, six months before his dictatorship came to an end. The dictator had already had thousands of Haitians and political opponents tortured and murdered, but it was his decision to have the daughters of a wealthy and highly-respected Dominican family shot and killed which gave rise to a wave of indignation in the US. The memory of the Mirabal sisters is cherished in the Dominican Republic, particularly that of Minerva who stood up bravely to the dictator: stamps bear her likeness, and several streets are named after her.

Mirabal sisters memorial

About 5km (3 miles) beyond Salcedo on the road to Tenares and set back slightly on the right-hand side is the **Museo de las Hermanas Mirabal** (9am–noon, 2–5pm, closed Monday, Tuesday), containing many photographs and personal belongings of the three sisters Patria, Minerva and Maria Teresa, who died aged 36, 33 and 25, including jewelry, clothing, a bloodstained handkerchief and the cap of their chauffeur who also died in the attack.

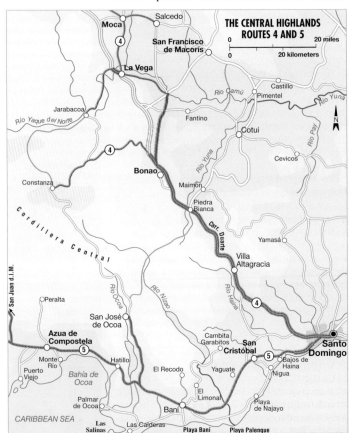

THE CENTRAL HIGHLANDS
ROUTES 4 AND 5

0   20 miles
0   20 kilometers

Salcedo
Moca
San Francisco de Macorís
La Vega
Castillo
Pimentel
Rio Camú
Rio Yuna
Jarabacoa
Fantino
Rio Yaque del Norte
Cotuí
Cevicos
Rio Pay
Bonao
Maimón
Constanza
Piedra Bianca
Rio Yuna
Cordillera Central
Yamasá
San Juan d.l.M.
Villa Altagracia
Carr. Duarte
Peralta
Rio Ocoa
Rio Nizao
Rio Haina
San José de Ocoa
Azua de Compostela
Cambita Garabitos
San Cristóbal
Santo Domingo
Monte Río
Hatillo
Yaguate
Bajos de Haina
Nigua
Puerto Viejo
Bahía de Ocoa
El Recodo
El Limonal
Playa de Najayo
Palmar de Ocoa
Bani
CARIBBEAN SEA
Las Salinas
Las Calderas
Playa Baní
Playa Palenque

Back in Moca, you can either drive to the Carretera Duarte to reach La Vega, or take the Carretera 21 and possibly connect it with excursions to the ruins of La Vega Vieja and to Santo Cerro (*see below*).

The town of **La Vega** (pop. 55,000), also known as La Concepción de La Vega, lies only a few miles south of the place where Columbus had a fortress built in 1495 during his search for gold. On 2 December 1562 the town of La Concepción that had sprung up around it was destroyed in a severe earthquake, and was only re-founded in the 17th century, this time to the west of the Río Camú. La Vega had its heyday when the railroad arrived here at the beginning of this century; its finest Victorian buildings, the Palacio de Justicia, the Teatro La Progresista and the Bombería (fire station), all date from that period. In 1992 the rather pompous Nueva Catedral (corner of Calle Independencia and Calle Restauración) was completed. The architect of this enormous concrete church was evidently inspired by the stepped towers of the High Middle Ages – their function was to transport workers and materials high above cities. The Biblical number 12 plays a role here, too: the building has 12 portals and 12 windows. Carnival time (*see page 75*) is the best time to visit La Vega; the celebrations here are longer, more colorful and also more 'devilish' than elsewhere.

An excursion can be made at this point from La Vega to the holy mountain of **Santo Cerro**, a center of pilgrimage. Take the Carretera Duarte 8km (5 miles) north and turn right at the small red signpost. A narrow asphalt track leads to a village with a church of early-colonial design but dating from 1886. Directly in front of it is a cross, and a tree next to it bears a plaque announcing that it came from the same tree Christopher Columbus used to make the first ever crucifix here. And thereby hangs a tale: in 1495 the Taínos rose up against their Spanish overlords on the Santo Cerro under the leadership of Guarionex. Just as they were about to set fire to the cross placed here by Columbus – so the story goes – the Virgen de las Mercedes appeared, protected the Christian symbol and forced the Indians to subjugate themselves. A section of the original cross is apparently preserved inside the church. It's certainly worth going round the back to enjoy the extraordinary ★ **view** across the valley, which Columbus named *La Vega Real* ('The Royal Meadows').

A steep section of road lined with statues of saints leads back down the other side of Santo Cerro and across to the Carretera 21 (the La Vega–Moca road). Turn left here in the direction of Pueblo Viejo. The houses of this village stand above the ruins of **La Vega Vieja**, a settlement originally founded by Columbus. A green signpost points left to the 'Ruinas Convento San Francisco'. A badly-sur-

Moca: Church of the Sacred Heart

53

Carnival masks

faced road lined with ramshackle huts leads for 2km (1 mile) to the remains of the Franciscan monastery, which was built in 1502. The foundation walls show the outlines of different sections of the first monastery built on American soil: the chapel, the well and the cloister. There is also a cemetery nearby.

Back on the Carretera 21, a signpost at the end of the village points the way to the **Fortaleza Nuestra Señora de la Concepción** – the fortress built by Columbus after his victory over the Taínos in 1495. One tower, with arrow-slits, is still quite well-preserved. A museum nearby contains several everyday items, both Taíno and Spanish, that were unearthed on the site.

On the road to Jarabacoa

To see a totally different kind of landscape, it's worth making a ★ **detour to Jarabacoa** (pop. 30,000; 526m/1,725ft). The distance there and back is 54km (33 miles), and the route leads along the foot of the Cordillera Central. Around 3km (2 miles) north of La Vega there's a turn-off the Carretera Duarte. The road's condition is good, and soon it starts to get very steep as it makes its way up the **Alpes Dominicanos**, a popular holiday destination for the island's inhabitants. After an 11-km (6-mile) drive the **Hotel Montaña**, built during the Trujillo era, appears on the left – just the place for a peaceful mountain holiday.

Nestling among pine forests and the valleys of the Río Yaque del Norte and Río Jimona, Jarabacoa enjoys springtime temperatures almost the whole year round. There are several natural sights to see here. One is the **Salto de Jimenoa** waterfall. The water cascades 20m (65ft) and you can take a refreshing shower underneath. The best way to get there is on a trip organised by one of the local hotels (Piñar Dorado, tel: 574 2820 or Rancho Baiguate, tel: 574 6890).

Another good place to visit is the 2-km (1-mile) distant **Balneario La Confluencia**, a natural swimming pool created by the confluence of the Río Yaque del Norte and the Río Jimenoa. The shallow water here is particularly popular with the Dominicans during holiday season, when several stalls serve open-air snacks. Or you could go on an excursion to **Salto de Baiguate**, a waterfall with a natural swimming pool. It can only be reached along a very rough track, so it's advisable to use either a jeep or a horse. Book your trip at the Hotel Rancho Baiguate.

It takes between two and four days to scale the nearby **Pico Duarte** (3,175m/10,416ft), the highest peak in the Caribbean. The Pico Duarte lies at the southern edge of the Parque Nacional Armando Bermúdez, which together with the Parque Nacional José Carmen Ramírez next door covers a total surface area of 1,530sq km (590sq miles) of rain forest.

★ *Detour to Constanza*

Frangipani

The direct route between Jarabacoa and Constanza is a
bumpy track. You could just make the rough ride, which
takes about 2½ hours, with a normal car. However, it is
more comfortable to drive back to the Autopista Duarte
and carry on in the direction of Santo Domingo (104km/64
miles round trip). About 33km (20 miles) beyond La Vega,
just as you're entering the village of El Abánico, the Carretera 12 branches off next to the Parador Los Quatro Vien-
tos hotel. This road snakes its way steeply up the mountain
to an altitude of 1,220m (4,000ft). In the valley below you
can see the Rincón Reservoir sparkling in the sunlight, and
eventually the fertile high plateau comes into view: a Garden of Eden with coffee plantations, exotic flowers and
fields planted with many kinds of vegetables. The mild
climate here means that even apples, strawberries and
peaches can be successfully cultivated.

Short cuts don't always pay **55**

Coffee beans

Constanza itself (1,100m/3,608ft above sea-level)
doesn't have a lot to offer. There are a few restaurants
and some small hotels, but the place is very quiet. In December and January it's quite common for temperatures
to sink below freezing. The nearby valleys and mountains
are ideal for hiking trips, and the waterfalls at Aguas
Blancas, around 10km (6 miles) to the south are also worth
a visit.

After this detour, the way back to Santo Domingo passes
via **Bonao** (pop. 50,000), capital of the province of Mon-
señor Nouel. The town lies just off the main road, but
there's no need to leave it to find out what Bonao is famous for: all kinds of ceramic and agricultural products
can be bought from stalls along the roadside. The nearby
'Falconbridge' nickel mine was the second-largest in the
world until 1988. From Bonao it's another 85km (52 miles)
back to Santo Domingo (*see page 18*).

Route 5

The Southwest

Santo Domingo – San Cristóbal – Baní – Azua de Compostela – Barahona – Pedernales (289km/179 miles)
See maps on pages 52 and 59

The Autopista Sánchez leads into the still very 'untouristy' southwest of the country. It's drier than the north, the vegetation isn't as green and is much sparser. Allow a week for the trip to Pedernales and back, because there is a lot to see: relics from the pre-Columbian era, the heritage of colonialism, sites of historic battles fought in the 19th century, most of them against the Haitians, the Jaragua National Park and, last but not least, mile upon mile of untouched, beautiful beaches, especially the section between Barahona and Pedernales.

Freedom-fighter Máximo Gómez remembered in Baní

Leave Santo Domingo and head west on the Malecón, which will take you straight to the four-lane Carretera Sánchez. Pass the entrance to the Bajos de Haina container terminal, cross the Río Haina, and travel another 25km (15 miles) or so to the town of **San Cristóbal** (pop. 30,000) on the Río Nigua, capital of the province of the same name. It's a busy market town and trading center, and is named after some fortifications built by Bartolomé Colón at the beginning of the 16th century to protect the gold discovered at the mouths of the Haina and Nigua rivers.

The town as we know it today was founded at the beginning of the 19th century. On 6 November 1844 San Cristóbal was the scene of an important moment in history: it was here that the Dominican revolutionary government ratified the country's first constitution. The town

Shoe-shine time in San Cristóbal

is also more notorious than famous for being the birthplace of Rafael Leónidas Trujillo y Molina (1891–1961), who as the dictator 'General Trujillo' ruled the Dominican Republic from 1930 to 1961. He heaped honors and honorary titles on to the town of his birth. One of Trujillo's legacies is the neoclassical church of **Parroquia de Nuestra Señora de Consolación**, which was built in 1946. Like the Town Hall (where the constitution was signed in 1844) it lies quite close to the Parque Central. Trujillo used this church for much self-glorification; the dictator's ornate chair still stands in front of the mahogany altar. Trujillo's corpse lay in state in the basement of this building for a short while following his assassination in 1961, but after local protests it was transferred to France. The burial vault of the Trujillo family, entered via a wrought-iron door, contains several other tombs and statues of saints. A memorial outside the church marks the presumed location of the house where the Generalissimo was born.

Parroquia de Nuestra Señora de Consolación

There are several examples of Trujillo's architectural legacy outside the town center, too. About 5km (3 miles) to the north in the direction of La Toma is his former country seat, Casa de la Caoba. This ruined villa, the first floor of which is made entirely of mahogany *(caoba)*, is located on a hill with a fine view of the surrounding landscape. A few miles to the north of the Casa Caoba, Trujillo had a swimming and bathing complex built, originally for private use; today anyone can swim in the Balneario La Toma.

57

Located on a rise to the west of the town is the Palacio del Cerro. This fortress-like palace, built in the 1950s, was never actually occupied by Trujillo. The elevator stuck regularly, and the dark frescoes by the Spanish painter Vela Zanetti were not to the dictator's taste. In 1979 the empty palace provided shelter for hurricane victims, but it has recently been restored to house a Trujillo museum.

San Cristóbal is a good starting-point for two excursions (though unfortunately the roads for both are very badly surfaced). The first is to the small town of **Nigua**, 11km (7 miles) south of San Cristóbal. The beach here is much like any other, but the highlights are the two ★ **sugar mills** dating from the colonial era. One of them, Boca de Nigua, is still partially intact. The mill, in which the sugar cane was crushed by a mill-wheel driven by oxen, can be clearly recognised, as can the boiling house with its hearths. The other factory, Diego Caballero, is a few minutes' walk further west, and is older; only a few foundation walls remain, but the setting is picturesque. Several signboards outline the methods involved in 18th-century sugar production.

Sugar mill

The second excursion from San Cristóbal is 14km (8 miles) to the south: the beach at **Najayo**, which is very

Salt diggers at Las Salinas

popular with the locals, and also the Playa Palenque 6km (4 miles) further west. There's an exciting atmosphere here at weekends in the numerous bars next to the beach. The locals are fond of wading into the water clutching their drinks and consuming them chest-deep.

The route now continues across the Río Nizao in the province of Peravia and via its capital **Baní** (pop. 40,000). The name is derived from an old Indian word meaning 'the town rich in water'. Thanks to this, agriculture plays an all-important role here. Sugar cane has been cultivated in the Baní region since the colonial era, but the first settlement was only established here in the 18th century, founded by immigrants from the Canary Islands who lived mainly off livestock production. Today Baní is a very clean and well-kept town with an attractive center. On the second story of the modern Town Hall there is a small museum (no fixed opening times) containing the personal belongings of Máximo Gómez, the Cuban freedom-fighter; he was born in Baní on 18 November 1836 and died on Castro Island in 1905. Another memorial to Máximo Gómez in Baní is easier to visit: the small park laid out in the Calle Máximo Gómez, with a statue of the freedom-fighter at its center.

Mural and monument to Gómez

One interesting excursion from Baní is a trip north (20km/12 miles) along the Río Baní via El Recodo to Limonal, where there's a great view across the Valdesia Reservoir. Those keen on crashing waves and flying spray should go to the **Playa Baní** 7km (4 miles) south of the town. There are more peaceful beaches with extensive dunes about 20km (12 miles) to the west in Las Calderas and also on the small ★ **Las Salinas Peninsula**, protected as a national monument, is named after the local salt-pans; the latter have grown very popular with windsurfers.

From Baní the Carretera 2 leads through increasingly barren-looking landscape. After 12km (7 miles) a road branches off northwards; those not in a hurry at this point can take a detour along a well-surfaced road (Carretera 41) to **San José de Ocoa** (pop. 25,000); 76km/47 miles there and back). Set in attractive, lush green landscape, San José was founded in the 17th century by several runaway slaves *(cimarrones)*. The pleasant, mild climate promotes the growth of fruit and vegetables around the town, particularly figs and potatoes.

After this detour into the 'cooler' regions, continue along the Carretera Sánchez to **Hatillo**. This little village lies at the foot of the mountain known as El Número, which in 1849 was the scene of the last battle between the Dominicans and the Haitians. General Duvergé's army inflicted such a heavy defeat on the Haitian troops here that they never dared set foot on Dominican soil again. From Hatillo a rough track leads south to the Bay of Ocoa with its shallow waters and attractive coral. The fishing village of **Palmar de Ocoa** attracts deep sea fishermen.

The provincial capital of **Azua de Compostela** (pop. 85,000) lies at the center of a prosperous and well-irrigated

Prosperous Azua de Compostela

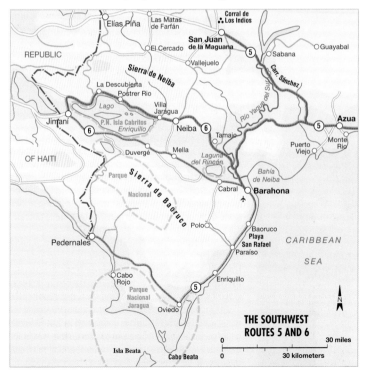

THE SOUTHWEST
ROUTES 5 AND 6

0   30 miles
0   30 kilometers

Pavilion in Parque Central

agricultural area. Melons are a particularly popular crop in this region of low precipitation. The town began as a settlement that was founded by Diego Velázquez in 1504, nearer the sea and 15km (9 miles) to the south. The harbor soon began competing with Santo Domingo, and Azua de Compostela was given its official charter in 1508. From 1505 to 1511 Hernán Cortés, who later conquered Mexico, was the town clerk here. Azua was actually destroyed by the French shortly afterwards in 1538, but then rebuilt. It was a tidal wave following an earthquake in 1791 that obliterated the town. Canarian settlers later rebuilt Azua on its present site. It was attacked by Haiti on several occasions during the Haitian-Dominican wars, and set ablaze in 1849 by the dictator Faustín Souloque's retreating troops after their defeat at El Número.

A monument stands in Azua's **Parque Central** in memory of the battle that took place on 19 March 1844 when the town successfully defended itself against attack by Haitian troops. Near the barracks there's another memorial to a different battle: it's in honor of the Indian chief Guarocuya, baptised Enriquillo, who put up successful resistance to the Spanish in this area and forced a peace agreement with the colonial forces in 1533. Many Azuanos are proud to be descended from the Taínos who settled this part of the island after the peace treaty.

The attractive beach at Azua, known as Monte Río (7km/4 miles southeast), is usually very crowded; those in search of solitude and tranquillity should avoid it.

In the old harbor of **Puerto Viejo**, 15km (9 miles) to the south, several remnants from the colonial period can be seen. To the north of Azua, the small mountain town of Peralta on the banks of the Río Jura, surrounded by coffee plantations, is most picturesque.

A worthwhile excursion from Azua is to the region around the town of **San Juan de la Maguana**. This is a thriving agricultural area, with many tobacco, rice and banana plantations. To the north of the attractive little town is a remnant of Indian culture, the Corral de los Indios. This reconstruction of a holy shrine consists of a gravestone with a carved face, surrounded by a stone circle.

Symbols of Barahona

On the trip from Azua to Barahona there are cacti as far as the eye can see, many of them with gorgeous flowers. On the western shore of the Bahía de Neiba the steppe-like landscape gradually changes into the fertile delta region of the Río Yaque del Sur, and soon **Barahona** (pop. 70,000) comes into view. This provincial capital lives mainly off its harbor, which is dominated by a sugar-mill. Other products shipped here include salt, wood, wax, minerals such as the semi-precious *larimar*, and agricultural produce. In 1997 a technical university was opened here.

Tourism is playing an increasingly important role in the town's economic life. The guests used to come exclusively from Santo Domingo; now they're arriving from all over the world. The new Maria Montez International Airport opened in 1996.

In the 17th century the Bay of Neiba, on which the town lies, was a favorite haunt of pirates; it was protected from the open sea by reefs and also virtually inaccessible by land. The notorious Cofresí is thought to have hidden here at one point. The town was founded by General Toussaint l'Ouverture who traveled eastwards from Haiti in 1802. It has quite a few wooden houses, and its church seems in danger of collapsing at any moment; otherwise there isn't much to see. The main meeting place for the locals is the Parque Central, where there are several restaurants and a disco. The long beach promenade is not very attractive, and the small municipal beach is polluted.

In contrast, beyond Barahona there is a beautiful section of coast road, which has recently been greatly improved. The broad, smooth asphalt road runs south; to the right are the foothills of the Baoruco Mountains, and to the left a series of deserted beaches and bays. About 10km (6 miles) futher on there's a left turn to the Playa El Qemaito, and after another 20km (12 miles) is the **Playa San Rafael**. A small stream meets the sea at the magnificent sandy beach here, so there's the choice between a freshwater or a seawater swim. Freshly-caught fish is served in the wooden huts. A word of warning: in bad weather, falling rock can be a hazard in this bay.

Carefree days

61

Continue now to Baoruco, with its large hotel complex, and then on to **Paraíso**. Located on a bay at the mouth of the Río Nizalta, the latter really is delightful. The beach promenade is lined by small terraced houses made of stone.

The stream at Playa San Rafael

Beyond Enriquillo the land starts getting flatter. Pastureland appears, and the towns and villages are farther apart. Beside the road on the left, just before the rather gloomy-looking village of Oviedo comes into view, is the administration building for the ★ **Parque Nacional Jaragua** (1,350sq km/521sq miles), the largest national park in the country. It covers the entire southern part of the Baoruco Peninsula, including the islands of Isla Beata and Alto Velo. This palm- and cactus-filled nature reserve contains several caves and the remains of Jaragua Indian settlements, after whom the park is named. The flora and fauna is incredibly varied. Over half of all the species of birds native to the island can be found here, including the almost extinct Hispaniola buzzard. There are several species of rare turtle, too The park may only be entered with a guide, and a permit obtainable from the central park administration in Santo Domingo (*see page 81*). Exploring this wild region on your own can be very dangerous, and is also punishable by a stiff fine.

King Palm

From Oviedo the Carretera 44 leads northwest in the direction of the Haitian border. After a 48-km (29-mile) drive with hardly anything coming in the opposite direction you'll see the turning to the small harbor and fishing village of **Cabo Rojo**. Those with plenty of time on their hands can ask their way to the **Playa Aguila**; its mile-long beaches are definitely worth the extra trip.

The town of **Pedernales**, capital of Pedernales province and not far from the border, has little of cultural interest to offer. It's famous for its bauxite, the raw material used to make aluminium. The municipal beach is unattractive, with no palm trees and therefore no shade. However the coast near the town seems to be very popular with divers and snorkelers.

Flamingoes

Route 6

Around Lake Enriquillo

Barahona – Neiba – Jimaní – Duvergé – Barahona (208km/129 miles) *See map on page 59*

One of the most attractive regions of the Dominican Republic is the area around Lake Enriquillo. The salt lake, surrounded by the mountains of the Sierra de Neiba and the Sierra de Baoruco, lies at the bottom of a natural basin almost 40m (130ft) below sea-level (the lowest point in the Caribbean). The region is hot and dry, though very fertile, too, thanks to numerous springs and small rivers. The temperatures are around 9°F (5°C) higher than the areas of the country close to the sea. The Sierra de Baoruco National Park has all kinds of different vegetation levels up to an altitude of 2,300m (7,500ft); there are more than 160 varieties of orchids and almost 50 species of bird, as well as rare butterflies. The driest zones contain not only cacti but also pine and even deciduous forests.

The road to Neiba

The starting-point for this tour is Barahona. Reliable guides can be found in the hotels; they take visitors to the main places of interest and point out the odd interesting detail in return for a small fee.

Leave Barahona (*see page 62*) on the Carretera 44 in a northwesterly direction, following it for 12km (7 miles) to the point where the Carretera 48 branches off to the left. Follow the 48 across the Río Yaque del Sur, the border of Baoruco Province; this region is full of sugar cane. Pass the small village of Tamayo and then cross the foothills of the Sierra de Neiba to reach **Neiba** (pop. 25,000), a friendly market town which is known for its grapes, sold on the main square in season.

Soon after the village of Villa Jaragua, the enormous **★★ Lake Enriquillo** comes into view for the first time. Its shallow salt water – three times saltier than the sea because of steady evaporation – lies immobile in the sunshine. The lake is what remains of an inlet that used to extend from the west coast of Haiti deep inside the interior of the island, but was then separated from the sea by movements of the earth's crust. The 'Lago' is 42km (26 miles) long and 12km (7 miles) wide. The lake bed is covered with a thick layer of ancient shells and fossilised coral.

Near Postrer Río, up on the right above the road, there are some remnants of Taíno culture in the **Caves of Las Caritas**. Those who feel strong enough to make the 50-m (164-ft) ascent will be rewarded by several very interesting scratch-marks on the cave walls resembling faces; some are only rough outlines, others are more detailed.

Lake Enriquillo

Caves of Las Caritas

Enriquillo, the Indian leader, and his men are thought to have sought refuge here from the Spanish. Strategically, the caves are well located: there's a view across the entire island from up here.

A few hundred yards away is the administration office of the ★★ **Parque Nacional Isla Cabritos**. The 'Isle of Goats', 12km (7 miles) long and 2km (1 mile) wide, is the largest of the three islands in the lake. Its remoteness has turned it into a natural paradise, supporting an abundance of wildlife. Flamingoes, giant iguanas and even alligators live here; the latter can be spotted most easily in the morning hours. From the park office it's possible to be taken by boat – assuming, that is, you have a permit from the central administration in Santo Domingo. These excursions, which are cheaper if organised through a tour operator (*see page 87*), are around four hours long; the trip from the mainland to the island takes 45 minutes. The two smaller islands in the lake are Barbarita and La Islita.

Descubierta

The next stop on this route is **Descubierta**, which is a green oasis surrounded by featureless desert. The reason it exists is the nearby swimming area (*balneario*) of 'Las Barias', with its lake fed by underground springs. This is a good place to sit and watch children swimming, clothing being washed and elderly people chatting away in the shade of the palm trees. Simple food is also served from a small palm-roofed kitchen.

The border town of **Jimaní** at the western end of the lake appears reasonably prosperous, but at the same time extremely quiet. The border post, 7km (4 miles) away, is a 'hive of inactivity': the soldiers look bored, and apart from the odd *tap-tap* (multi-colored Haitian bus) bringing day-workers to the border and back from Haiti, there's nothing much going on.

The Carretera 46 follows the southern shore of the lake. Just before Duvergé on the left is the small *balneario* of 'La Zurza'; 5km (3 miles) beyond the village there's a turning to Neiba. At the intersection is the imposing-looking memorial to the Taíno chieftain Enriquillo, 'the first fighter for independence in the New World', who struggled against the Spanish colonists for 14 years (*see page 13*).

Enriquillo

Continue now via Mella in the direction of Cabral. The **Laguna del Rincón**, a 5-m (16-ft) deep freshwater lake extending across an area of 30sq km (12sq miles), comes into view on the left-hand side before you get there; it is home to innumerable flamingoes and cormorants, and also turtles (*jicotea*). The Laguna del Rincón is the second-largest lake in the country, and is fed by small streams and rainwater. The starting-point of this route, Barahona, is now only a few miles away.

Route 7

From Sugar to Tourism

Santo Domingo – Boca Chica – San Pedro de Macorís
– La Romana (102km/63 miles)

The southeast coast of the country is relatively densely populated, with a lot of tourist development. In contrast to the southwest this region has quite a few high-standard hotels, and remote and isolated beaches are something of a rarity. The main source of income for this part of the Dominican Republic is the sugar industry (the reason why San Pedro de Macorís became so prosperous during the 19th century), and things look set to remain that way for some time even though tourism is increasing very rapidly. The drive to La Romana can be done in a day.

Souvenirs at Boca Chica

Take the four-lane Autopista de las Américas eastwards from Santo Domingo; the highway's name derives from the 21 alphabetically-arranged, rather battered plaques along the side of the road bearing the names of the 21 countries of Latin America.

In **La Caleta**, 20km (12 miles) into the trip, a road branches off to Las Américas Airport, the largest in the country. Right on this intersection there's a park with an

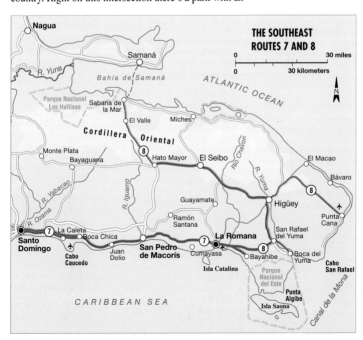

THE SOUTHEAST
ROUTES 7 AND 8

0 _____ 30 miles
0 _____ 30 kilometers

Nagua

R. Yuna

Samaná

Bahía de Samaná

ATLANTIC OCEAN

Parque Nacional
Los Haitises

Sabana de
la Mar

El Valle   Miches

Cordillera   Oriental

Monte Plata

Bayaguana

Hato Mayor   El Seibo   El Macao

Río Chavón   R. Yuma   Bávaro

R. Yabacao

R. Iguamo

R. Ozama

Guayamate   Higüey

Ramón   Santana   La Romana   Punta Cana

La Caleta   San Rafael del Yuma

Santo Domingo   Boca Chica

Cabo Caucedo   Juan Dolio   San Pedro de Macorís   Cumayasa   Bayahibe   Boca del Yuma

Isla Catalina   Parque Nacional del Este   Cabo San Rafael

CARIBBEAN SEA   Punta Algibe

Isla Saona   Canal de la Mona

interesting if rather grisly museum, the ★ **Museo Panteón** (10am–5pm, closed Sunday, Monday). It contains the skeletons of several Taíno Indians, buried in the 'embryonic' position (in contrast to Spanish dead who were buried with their hands clasped across their chests). The 31 skeletons here include a prosperous Taíno and his wife; according to custom, wives of highly-respected members of the Taíno Indian community were buried alive beside their husbands. The museum also contains several funerary gifts and other artefacts.

Off the harbor at La Caleta, the hulks two wrecked ships were sunk in order to create an artificial reef. Boats now take divers out to this protected underwater area, known as the ★ **Parque Submarino**; its banks of coral are home to numerous colorful species of tropical fish.

Hotel La Hamaca in Boca Chica has its own private beach

Travel along the Carretera Mella to the European-style tourist resort of **Boca Chica**. This is one of the least restful places on the island; the streets are full of hawkers, and the beach – even though attractive – is so full at weekends that it's hard to find a space to yourself. It was Trujillo who first made this place famous when he had a hotel built beside the beach. Known as 'the largest swimming pool in the Caribbean', this reef-protected bay – ideal for family fun and a variety of watersports – is never deeper than 1.5m (5ft). Today, Boca Chica with all its high-rise hotels and restaurants is probably the noisiest resort on the island – perfect for those whose ideal holiday involves non-stop nightlife and very little sleep.

Continue past the quiet beach of Guayacanes to Juan Dolio. There aren't any sights to see in this modern resort, which has become a center of package-holiday tourism in the past few years, but diving and windsurfing courses are available.

Beach craft at Boca Chica

It's only another 15km (9 miles) now from Juan Dolio to **San Pedro de Macorís** (pop. 90,000), the fourth-largest town in the country and named after the Macorís Indians who once populated this region. San Pedro lies at the mouth of the Río Iguamo, which is spanned here by a massive bridge. Keep right on the other side of the bridge and you'll arrive at the center of this town, founded in 1822. There is a *zona franca* (free-trade zone) here, and agriculture also plays an important role. Sugar cane isn't as important as it used to be; at the beginning of this century San Pedro was the center of the Dominican sugar industry. Hundreds of miles of railroad connected the sugar factories across the country with its harbor. When the world sugar price increased sharply after World War I, San Pedro became incredibly prosperous.

There are few visible remnants of that time of glory in the town today, but those that do remain are still worth a visit. From the Parque Duarte, walk westwards along the Avenida Independencia (or along the parallel Calle Duarte) in the direction of the river promenade and several architectural jewels of the good old days will come into view: the Victorian-style **fire station** on the Calle Duarte, for instance, which was built by the Hamburg-America line between 1903 and 1906; or the former **Parliament Building** on the corner of Duarte and Sánchez, today an ironmonger's. On the river promenade at the end of the Avenida Independencia is the striking-looking church of **San Pedro Apóstol** (1908–13). The tower is decorated with Gothic-style gargoyles, and there's also a medieval-looking rose window. The three-aisled interior contains an elaborately carved mahogany altar. San Pedro de Macorís's close links with its past are nowhere more evident than in the festival of St Peter, held every 29 June; the celebrations feature dances known as *gouloyas*, which date back to African rites and were brought over by laborers employed in the British Antilles (*see page 75*). Known familiarly as *cocolos*, these workers were needed because the local population was unable to cope with the sheer amount of labor involved in the sugar harvest.

The Carretera 3 now leads eastwards, passing the baseball stadium of Tetelo-Vargas, where the municipal market has established itself opposite. On the outskirts of the town turn left, and continue into open countryside past pastureland and sugar cane plantations.

Beyond the rivers Soco and Cumayasa (there's a small road leading to the attractive beach at Cumayasa just before the bridge) is the provincial capital of **La Romana** (pop. 100,000). The enormous 'Central de La Romana' sugar mill, the largest employer in these parts, can be seen from far and wide. La Romana only began to develop in

San Pedro's fire station

67

San Pedro Apóstol

Souvenirs of La Romana

Altos de Chavón

Shady verandahs

Plying the Río Chavón

The amphitheater

the mid-19th century, and it owes much of its prosperity to Cuban sugar producers and also to the North American Gulf & Western Company, which bought up vast tracts of land for sugar-cane cultivation during the 1920s.

The small park with its obelisks in the Avenida Libertad is a haven of tranquillity in the busy town. The brightly-painted wooden houses in this quarter belong to the more wealthy employees of the sugar trade. The areas round the town center are poorer. The Parque Central has its usual town hall and parish church; above the church is the Mercado Municipal, an entire district full of stores and stalls where it's very easy to get lost.

It's just a 20-minute boat trip from La Romana's small harbor to the Isla Catalina. The beaches have fine, white sand with some of the best bathing in waters protected by reefs. Diving is also excellent, but there is no need to get your feet wet if you don't want to: the diving grounds can also be admired through glass-bottomed boats.

The sports center of Casa de Campo on the eastern edge of town also has a fascinating cultural sight: the ★★ **Altos de Chavón**, a 16th-century Mediterranean village situated on a hill above the Río Chavón with a great panoramic view. There's the small church of San Estanislao, an **amphitheater** with a seating capacity of 3,000 and an ★ **archaeological museum** (8am–9pm) with some fascinating exhibits documenting the Taíno culture. The complex also contains a School of Design – a branch of the Parsons School in New York. Scholarship holders from all over the world can study here in a uniquely beautiful environment. There are galleries, craft stores, and restaurants of all kinds. Altos de Chavín is open to everyone and definitely worth a visit; note, however, that the food and drink prices are somewhat higher here than they are elsewhere on the island.

Route 8

The Natural Beauties of the Southeast

La Romana – Higüey – Sabana de la Mar (169km/105 miles) *See map on page 65*

The highlights of this route include the crystal-clear blue waters of the Parque Nacional del Este with its fascinating island of Saona, the pilgrimage town of Higüey, and the sleepy little town of Sabana de la Mar with its optional detour to the Samaná Peninsula or to the Los Haïtises National Park. The remote beaches near the comfortable resorts of Punta Cana or Bávaro Beach make a good detour for fans of sun and sand. The La Romana–Samaná route can be done in a day; those eager to visit and enjoy the eastern beaches should plan a night's stay.

Follow the main road from La Romana in the direction of San Rafael de Yuma. After 8km (5 miles) the road crosses an impressive ravine, with the Río Chavón far below. Another 5km (3 miles) on take the right turn to Bayahibe. On the way, to the left, is the Amazonia restaurant where the owner has set up a miniature zoo with various types of parrot, monkey and wild cats.

Beach babe at Bayahibe

    The town of **Bayahibe**, founded by Puerto Ricans, was once a quiet fishing village. Today it's a meeting-place for independent travellers, attracted by the great beach, cafés and restaurants and a good choice of private accommodation as well as a recently opened luxury hotel. Bayahibe is the starting-point for the highly recommended excursion to the ★★ **Isla Saona** (pop. 1,000). Catamarans (to the island's main beach) or speedboats take visitors across to this island (117sq m/140sq yds), which forms part of the Parque Nacional del Este. The boat trip passes untouched beaches and mangrove forests, finally reaching the island about two hours later. The largest settlement on Saona, Mano Juan, has a monument to the man who discovered it: Jerónimo Anari. He is said to have landed here on 14 October 1495, named the island *Bella Saona* (after the Italian town of Savona), planted a tree, set up a cross and erected a gallows.

Boats to Isla Saona

Back on the main road, the next destination is **San Rafael de Yuma.** Just at the entrance to the town a bumpy track leads off to the left, arriving 2km (1 mile) further on at the only sight this town has to offer: the **Casa Fuerte de Ponce de Léon.** It was from this fortress-like house between 1505 and 1508 that General Ponce de Léon directed the conquest of the eastern part of the island and also founded Higüey. He left on his voyages to Puerto Rico and

San Rafael de Yuma: Casa Fuerte

Florida from the nearby harbor of Boca de Yuma. The house still contains several interesting items of 16th-century furniture.

Roughly 10km (6 miles) to the east, ★ **Boca de Yuma** lies on a rock projecting out into the ocean. The sea is rich in fish here, at the estuary of the Río Yuma. In June, deep-sea fishermen converge on this area to take part in an angling competition. There are several caverns along the rocky coast that can only be explored in the company of a guide.

Continue for another 48km (29 miles) from San Rafael de Yuma across flat grazing land to reach the provincial capital of **Higüey** (pop. 40,000), founded in the early 16th century. Soon afterwards it became a center of pilgrimage when two Spanish soldiers brought a miracle-working painting of the Virgin Mary here. A church was built between 1512 and 1572 to house the picture (and was rebuilt in 1881 after destruction in an earthquake). Pilgrims have been visiting this church each year on 21 January since the late 17th century to commemorate the Spanish victory over the French at the battle of Limonada, fought on that day in 1691. The success is attributed to Nuestra Señora de Altagracia in Higüey, and she has been the country's official patron saint since 1922.

Higüey: old and new cathedrals

When the Old Cathedral in the town center could no longer accommodate the vast number of pilgrims, a ★ **New Cathedral** was built nearby between 1952 and 1971. This mighty concrete structure with its tower reminiscent of a jawbone is entered through a door decorated with copper plate, bearing reliefs of the Miracle of Higüey. The statue of the virgin and a silver crown are in a glass case on the altar.

Punta Cana Beach

To the east of Higüey on the coast is a row of comfortable holiday villages with attractive beaches which unfortunately can only be reached along lengthy and, in places, very arduous roads. They include the Bávaro Beach Resort and the Punta Cana Beach Resort. Those who book their holidays here are definitely 'birds in gilded cages'. At the **Manatí Park** (on the main road close to Fiesta Bávaro) sea-cows (manatees) and other animals threatened by extinction are bred; other attractions include dolphin shows, flying tamed parrots and 'dancing horses'.

From Higüey the route continues westwards along the Carretera 4. The small town of El Seibo, rebuilt after the earthquake of 1751, is surrounded by cocoa and banana plantations. Another 24km (14 miles) to the west is **Hato Mayor**, a market town and provincial capital well-known for its cattle breeding (the name means 'large pasture').

Apart from its attractive park of Mercé de la Roja, the town has little to offer in the way of sights.

Carry on northwards now from Hato Mayor on the Carretera 103 through a hilly tropical landscape. The rather dreary town of **Sabana de la Mar** lives off two things: the ferry traffic to and from Samaná (*see page 44*), which finances several of the local restaurants and stores, and also the boat trips from here to the ★★ **Parque Nacional Los Haïtises** organized by the park administration. The excursions are mainly to the coastal zone of the park, which covers an overall area of 208sq km (80sq miles). Inland, the dense mangrove jungle gradually turns into near-impenetrable tropical rain forest. Inside the limestone islands, huge caves, many as much as 300m (1,000ft) high, have been created by millions of years of rainfall. Some of the caves contain pictorial evidence of Taíno habitation. Today the park is one of the most important reserves of flora and fauna in the country.

Coconut palm

71

The beach at Sabana de la Mar is not suitable for bathing; instead it's better to travel 40km (24 miles) further on along the badly-surfaced Carretera 104 to **Miches** (allow 90 minutes for the trip). The magnificent coast here is ideal for swimming, diving or sailing. The 'Reserva Científica Lagunas Redonda y Limón' nature reserve (101sq km/39sq miles) a few miles east of Miches is virtually inaccessible, and should be explored with the help of a guide. This unique bird sanctuary contains two lagoons that are just 1.5m (5ft) deep; the Laguna Redonda is the only one connected to the sea.

Traveling any further east along the coast from this point is not recommended, because of the poor condition of the roads.

Heron in mangroves

A Diverse Heritage

Opposite: 'Morning stroll' by Candido Bido

Dominican culture is the result of an intermingling of various elements over the centuries: Indian, Spanish, African and American in particular. This mixture appears in various combinations across the Caribbean, and has resulted in a Creole culture with which many of the islanders happily identify.

Indian inheritance

The artistically and socially highly-developed Taíno Indian tribes constitute the cradle of Creole culture. Although they were almost completely exterminated just a few decades after the arrival of the Spanish, elements of their culture lived on in local architecture, language and cuisine. Today *casabe* bread is still baked according to the old Taíno recipe, and wooden houses with thatched roofs and covered verandahs, based on the Indian *bohio* huts, are still built. Words like *tabaco* (tobacco), *huracán* (hurricane) and *canoa* (canoe) are all pre-Hispanic, too.

Bohio-style hut

Spanish influence

73

Cultural life was far more strongly influenced by the Spanish. Literature and the arts largely reflected European styles. It was only from the mid-19th century onwards that any kind of 'national' style emerged. A Caribbean *modernismo* at the end of the 19th century was followed by relatively radical movements such as *postumismo*, which called all past artistic traditions into question and was related to the *Dada* movement in Europe, or *costumbrismo* which, though conventionally impressionistic in its formal language, insisted on the representation of Dominican themes alone. However, these and other attempts at cultural independence were repressed under the US occupation (1916–24) and the Trujillo regime (1930–61).

Merengue – the national music

Merengue has taken over

From the moment you land in the Dominican Republic there's a constant companion: *merengue*, the national music. There's a live combo at the airport, and taped music can be heard on the radio in the taxi, at the hotel, in the bar, on the beach – everywhere. Dozens of small radio stations ensure that *merengue* is rarely out of earshot.

This fast music in 2/4 time and the dance of the same name (where the dancers hold each other closely and sway their hips a lot, though less obviously than in the *lambada*) first conquered the country in the early years of the 19th century, and probably originated in Cuba. Initial reactions to *merengue* were negative. Many Dominicans would have preferred to stick with their traditional dances such as the *tumba* or the *contradanza*. It was the young people who fell for the new and very obviously 'physical' dancing style. *Merengue* soon became highly popular in the Caribbean and in South America, and has remained so.

Traditionally, *merengue* music is played by a three-man combo known as the *perico ripiao* (literally: parrot fricassé). The instruments are either a *tres* or a *cuatro* (two kinds of guitar-like stringed instruments), a *tambora* (a large two-sided drum) and the *güiro* (a calabash with notches that is rubbed with a stick). At the end of the 19th century the stringed instruments were replaced by the accordion, introduced by European sailors. Today it's rare to hear *merengue* in this combination, however. Electronics have taken over here, too: the accordion has made way for the keyboard, an electric bass guitar has replaced the rhythmic backing from the drum, the melody is played on alto-saxophone and the metallic *guayo* has taken over from the *güiro*. All this is often accompanied by a three-part brass section. The lyrics used to contain a lot of social criticism, but have now been largely tailored to suit harmless contemporary tastes in pop music.

Pop idols

To get an idea of just how enthusiastic the Dominicans are when it comes to music, observe Santo Domingo at the end of July and beginning of August each year. That's when the whole town celebrates its Merengue Festival, and is transformed into one enormous open-air disco.

Alongside the *merengue* there are several dances of African origin on the island, such as the *mangulina*, a circular dance, or the *carabíne*, which originated during the struggle against the Haitians and is accompanied by a three-man band known as a *pripi*.

An abstract work

Today's cultural variety

Following a phase of political consolidation in the 1960s and 1970s, art in the Dominican Republic is gradually reverting to African and Indian roots. The Creole cultural movement known as *criollismo* is finding many adherents, especially in Santo Domingo.

Clara Sofia Florez: Descubrimento

In painting there has been a move towards connecting Indian symbolism with African color and expressiveness. The epic literature reflects strong anti-American sentiment; it is clear that the Dominicans are loath to abandon their hard-won cultural identity.

Controversial themes are no longer taboo. Women's role in a male-dominated society, the function of language and its dialects in self-realisation, the effects of increasing technology on community life, and the social conflict between rich and poor all find reflection in art.

More cultural centers are appearing in the towns, and small independent theaters, art galleries and literary groups are being formed. Creole culture is rapidly becoming an independent lifestyle expression in its own right.

Festivals and Folklore

Judging from the number of official festivals throughout the year, the Dominicans don't appear to be all that fun-loving. Don't be deceived, though: fun needs no official occasion here. In addition to the Merengue festivals (*page 73–4*), the majority of the population celebrates all the major Catholic festivals, and the voodoo supporters (*see page 12*) celebrate their saints as well. On top of all that, however, there's carnival time.

A young merengue fan

The Dominicans are so passionate about carnivals that they have two: on **National Day** (27 February) and on **Restoration Day** (16 August). The carnival festivities were introduced by the Spanish but are also strongly influenced by African culture; the *diabolos*, or 'devils', who play an important role, are dressed differently in each region and wear very frightening masks. In Santo Domingo the devils are always played by men; in Santiago the *lechones* (devils with pigs' bladders tied around them) descend on the La Joya and Los Pepines suburbs; in Monte Cristi the *toros* (jesters dressed as bulls) tend to attack innocent passers-by. The devils also chase evil spirits out of the island's cemeteries by cracking whips loudly.

African influence in the Republic is most strongly felt in San Pedro de Macorís, where the *gouloyas* – jesters playing cymbals and dressed in smocks adorned with mirrors – dance through the streets to the rhythmic accompaniment of African music. They symbolize the uprising of the slaves against their oppressors.

Another very popular pursuit, especially in the smaller villages in rural areas, is cockfighting. These fights take place every Sunday in circular wooden arenas known as *gallere*. Every village has its *Club Gallístico*, or cockfighting club.

Carnival masks

Food and Drink

The local cuisine, *comida criolla*, has many roots; culinary traces have been left here not only by the Spanish colonizers but also by later immigrants and the tourist trade.

The Dominican equivalent of 'Montezuma's Revenge' is 'Caonabo's Revenge', and although Caonabo can sometimes strike this should still not limit tourists to the luxury restaurants alone. As long as those with sensitive stomachs avoid eating unpeeled fruit and green salads, they can easily eat wherever the Dominicans eat – in a *restaurante criollo*, for instance, one of those small, tidy-looking restaurants where there's usually a choice of international as well as local specialities.

It's cheaper and also even more 'Dominican' to eat in the so-called *comedores*. These simple restaurants can be found on every street corner, and as a rule there's no menu; instead the dishes are presented inside a glass counter, which also makes ordering exceptionally simple – all you have to do is point.

On trips into the interior, *paradas* are good places to eat; located on most of the main routes, they're like *comedores*, only somewhat larger and more impersonal. Locals can often be seen peddling small and delicious snacks for travelers at many of the major traffic intersections and overland bus-stops: peeled oranges, sections of pineapple, peanuts, candy and highly colorful types of lemonade. Snacks such as sandwiches, desserts *(dulces)* and various drinks can be purchased in the numerous *cafeterías* and also in the *colmados*, grocery stores which seem to sell nearly everything and usually have a few chairs and tables handy.

Banana fritters
Colmados offer snacks

A typical breakfast consists of sandwiches, fresh fruit and fried eggs. Dominicans tend to eat supper far later than Europeans. Classic main courses include *locrio*, a variant of paella allegedly invented by Spanish women when European ingredients were not available. The stew known as *sancocho* contains either chicken *(sancocho de pollo)* or various other kinds of meat *(sancocho prieto)*. The ingredients, which can include maize, pumpkin and yam, tend to vary with the region and the cook involved. The most popular dish is definitely *Bandera Dominicana*, consisting of fried meat, beans and rice. It is usually accompanied by *tostones* or *fritos verdes* (strips of fried green banana) and salad. Several restaurants and wayside snack bars provide marinated pieces of pork crackling *(chicharones)* or of chicken *(chicharones de pollo)*, which make ideal snacks between meals.

Regional specialities are best tried out in the areas themselves. In Monte Cristi and Azua there's *chivo guisado*, goat stewed in a mixture of onions, rum and red wine; and

Seafood dishes are always available

Coconuts on the roadside

Quality rum

Fresh ingredients at the market

the Samaná Peninsula produces the delicious *pescado con coco*, fish cooked in coconut milk sauce. Although the Dominicans tend to favor meat over fish, seafood dishes are always available in the coastal areas. One speciality with allegedly aphrodisiac properties (though not for the squeamish) is *lambí*, the boiled hide of a large sea snail. The recipe for *casabe*, bread baked on a stone slab, dates back to the Taínos. *Yaniqueques*, pancakes fried in oil, were introduced by the *Cocolos*, the name given to immigrants from the English-speaking West Indian islands. Another absolutely delicious dessert is *coco nuevo con leche*, prepared from fresh coconut.

In the tropical heat fruit juices, or *jugos*, go a long way towards quenching thirst. The juice of various exotic fruits is usually freshly squeezed, or mixed with milk *(batida)*. *Refrescos* (lemonades) can be very strongly sweetened. Mountains of unripe green coconuts can often be seen at roadside vendors' stands. Their milk is known as *agua de coco* and is most refreshing.

Beer *(cerveza)* is served ice-cold all over the Dominican Republic. The local brand, 'Presidente' is very popular with Americans and Europeans, but the Dominicans prefer stronger varieties such as 'Quisqueya' or 'Bohemia'. The most popular and also the most traditional alcoholic beverage on the island is, of course, rum *(ron)*. It can be drunk straight or on the rocks, or with Cola or Sprite – though the proportion of rum to whatever it gets mixed with is always distinctly high. Good drinks at sunset include *Piña Colada* (rum and pineapple juice), *Batida de Coco* (rum and coconut milk) and *Daiquiri* (rum and lemon juice). The most famous rum manufacturers are Barceló, Brugal, Bermúdez, Siboney and Macorix; the best-quality rum is to be found in bottles bearing the words *añejo* (aged) or *Reserva Especial*.

Restaurant selection

The following suggestions from the Dominican Republic's main centers are listed according to three categories: $$$ = expensive; $$ = moderate: $ = inexpensive.

Cabarete
$$Leandro's, tel: 571 0713. Creole-style seafood.

Las Terenas
$$Paco Cabaña, tel: 240 6300. Seafood. **$La Salsa**, Pueblo Pescadores at the beach, tel: 240 6049. French-run restaurant with beautiful terrace. **$Casa Azul**, opposite police station. Local and international dishes.

Puerto Plata
$$Titanic, Avenida Malecón, tel: 586 2588. New restaurant with nautical theme. **$$Acuarela**, Calle Professor Certad 3, junction Pres. Vásquez. Best restaurant in town.

Samaná
$$L'Hacienda, Malecón, tel: 538 2383. Famous for its kebabs and barbecues. **$Café de Paris**, Malecón, tel: 538 2488. Pizza and crêpes, cocktails in the evening.

Santiago de los Caballeros
$$Pez Dorado, Calle del Sol 43, tel: 582 2518. Best Creole and international food in town. **$$El Café**, Avenida Texas, Los Jardinio, tel: 587 4247. Small, pleasant restaurant, serving excellent international cuisine.

Santo Domingo
$$$Fonda La Atarazana, Calle Atarazana 5, tel: 689 2900. Dominican cuisine. **$$$ La Briciola**, Arzobispo Meriño 152, tel: 688 5055. Excellent food in colonial setting. **$$$Pat'e Palo**, Calle Atarazana 25, tel: 687 8089. Waiters dressed as pirates serve good quality French-Italian dishes. **$$$Mesón de la Cava**, in a natural cave in Mirador del Sur Park, tel: 533 2818. Creole cuisine, dancing. **$$$Sully**, Charles Summers y Calle Caoba, tel: 562 3389. Excellent seafood some distance from center. **$$América**, Santomé/Arzobispo Nouel, tel: 682 7194. International cooking; **$Meson de Bari**, Calle Hostos, junction Salome Ureña. Local meeting place of academics and artists, where simple but delicious dishes are served till 9pm.

Sosúa
$$El Atlántico, in Los Charamicos. Romantic atmosphere on the cliffs. **$$La Puntilla**, tel: 571 2215. Sea view from the former summer home of an American diplomat; **$$Marco Polo**, Calle Dr. Alejo Martinez, tel: 571 3680. Well run restaurant with terrace high above the sea.

Cafés double as stores

79

Preparing fish

Active Holidays

Fine white sand, turquoise sea, soft green palm trees and not a cloud in the sky – like most islands in the Antilles, the Dominican Republic is ideal for all kinds of sporting pursuits, on the land as well as in and on the water. The hotels in the larger beach resorts all offer numerous opportunities to practise or to learn sports, and if they don't do exactly what's required they will be able to provide the address of somewhere that does.

Predator of the deep

Diving

The astonishingly colorful and varied undersea flora and fauna isn't the only attraction for divers: there are also somewhere in the region of 400 wrecked ships lying off the coast of Hispaniola, some of them five centuries old, plus lost anchors and cannons – it's a veritable underwater museum. The south of the island is better for diving because the Caribbean tends to be calmer than the Atlantic with its sharp winds, though local professional divers have their favorite areas on both the north and the south coasts.

Coral is protected

In the Parque Submarino La Caleta, around 20km (12 miles) east of Santo Domingo, a wrecked ship has been sunk to create an artificial reef. La Caleta is considered a first-class diving ground and has coral, sponges and several very colorful species of fish. To the west of the capital, divers should try the area around the delta of the Río Haina, where salt and freshwater mix, as well as the coast off Palenque where there is a wrecked ship dating from 1806. The still relatively unexplored reefs and caves around the Isla Beata are home to numerous fascinating examples of undersea flora and fauna.

In the north the enormous coral reef known as Silver Banks, 140km (85 miles) to the northeast of Puerto Plata, and also the Bay of Samaná are both excellent destinations for divers.

For more information contact: Actividades Acuáticas, Santo Domingo, tel: 688 5838, Puerto Plata tel: 320 2567.

There are good diving schools in almost all the larger tourist resorts (e.g. D.I.V.E. Samaná in Las Galeras or Treasure Divers in Boca Chica)

Cabarete

Windsurfing, waterskiing and sailing

The very best place for windsurfers is the village of Cabarete on the north coast. The small bay is protected by a reef, and the wind and wave conditions here are held in high regard by the world's top professionals. For beginners, there are more than a dozen windsurfing schools to choose from.

Waterskiing is provided by many of the larger beach hotels in, for example, Punta Cana, Playa Dorada (Puerto

Plata), Boca Chica, Juan Dolio and La Romana (Casa de Campo). For parasailing the place to go is the Playa Dorada in Puerto Plata. For more information contact Actividades Acuáticas, Puerto Plata, tel: 320 2567, Boca Chica, tel: 523 4511. Catamarans, yachts and smaller boats can be hired at many of the resorts, too.

Small boats can be hired

Deep sea fishing

Fishing competitions are held annually, the catch being blue marlin, bonito and dorado. In June a competition is staged near Boca de Yuma, the most popular deep sea fishing area. For more information contact the nearest Club Nautico (for the club in Santo Domingo, tel: 586 3988).

Golf

The luxurious holiday village of Casa de Campo near La Romana has three 18-hole courses; one, known as 'Teeth of a Dog', is among the best in the world. To the west of the capital there is the Santo Domingo country club; in Santiago the Las Aromas Golf Club; in Juan Dolio the METRO Country Club; in Punta Cana the Bavaro Beach Club. The Playa Dorada Hotel in Puerto Plata has a course and there's another at the Playa Grande. Nine-hole courses include: Costambar Golf Club (Puerto Plata) and Loma de Chivo (Samaná Peninsula), Quintas de Primavera (Jarabacoa). For more information: Golf Guide Info Office, tel: 248 5263.

81

Riding and polo

Many hotels as well as tour operators provide horses for riding into the surrounding area. The most common local breed is called *Paso-Fino*, or 'gentle step', and they really are easy to ride. The Casa de Campo Hotel has several polo fields; games can be watched during the season (November to May) and lessons are provided as well. Those keen on betting can try their luck at the 'Hipódromo Quinto Centenario' race-course near Santo Domingo.

The Sierra de Neiba in the southwest

Hiking and mountaineering

The hiking center of the Dominican Republic is Jarabacoa, located in the Central Highlands. With their year-round spring temperatures, the pine forests are marvelously refreshing places to hike. Climbing the highest peak in the Caribbean, the Pico Duarte (3,175m/10,416ft) at the southern edge of the Armando Bermúdes National Park, is also worth the effort.

An excursion like this is best organized via Ecoturisa in Santo Domingo, tel: 221 4104/5/6, or the Direccion Nacional de Parques, Santo Domingo, Av. Independencia 359, tel: 682 5072 and 685 1316, who will provide experienced guides and the necessary park permits.

Getting There

By air

The Dominican Republic is served by the major American, European and Latin American airlines, and a number of Caribbean-island operators. There are international airports at Santo Domingo (south coast), Puerto Plata (north coast), Punta Cana (east coast), Barahona (south coast) and Samaná (north coast). On arrival and departure an airport tax of US$10 has to be paid.

From the US
American Airlines (daily from Boston, Miami, New York and San Juan, Puerto Rico), tel: 800-433 7300.
Continental (daily from Newark, New Jersey), tel: 800-231 0856.
TWA (from Boston, Los Angeles, New York and Florida), tel: 800-892 4141.
Northwest Airlines and several charter operators also run services to the Dominican Republic.

From Europe
Several airlines fly to Latin America from Europe with onward or connecting flights to the Dominican Republic, including (with reservations telephone numbers):
Air France (twice a week from London via Paris), tel: 020 8759 2311.
Alitalia (twice a week from London via Rome), tel: 020 7602 7111.
American Airlines (daily from London via Boston or Miami), tel: 0345 789789.
Continental (daily from London and Manchester via Newark, New Jersey), tel: 01293 827411.
Iberia (five times a week from London via Madrid on Iberia, Viasa and/or Aerolineas), tel: 020 7830 0011, ask for 'Latin Savers'.
TAP Air Portugal (once a week from London via Lisbon), tel: 020 7828 0262.

The Dominican Republic is an increasingly popular charter destination. See your local travel agent for details about package vacations which usually include flights, airport transfers and accommodation.

By sea

There are cargo and passenger shipping services operating from New York, New Orleans, Miami and South American countries. Several cruise lines from the US, Canada and Europe include the Dominican Republic on their itineraries. Details from the Republic's tourist offices in the country concerned.

83

Three on a motoconcho

Getting Around

By car and motorbike

A popular mode of transport

The main north-south route, the Autopista Duarte, from Santo Domingo to Santiago is a motorway; the other main roads along the north and south coasts are also well surfaced. In other parts of the country, and especially on side roads, potholes and other surface damage have to be reckoned with. Routes which look quite important on maps often turn out to be nothing more than bumpy dirt tracks that are sometimes closed depending on the season. This is particularly true of the interior. Ask the locals which route they would recommend. Signposting is poor and you may have to ask the way as you go. Animals wandering about or lying in the road are another hazard.

Look out for 'sleeping policemen'

Near police stations, schools, barracks and at intersections in towns and villages, look out for the *policía acostado* ('sleeping policemen'). They can often be extremely abrupt and not even the locals always spot them in time. Beware!

The maximum speed allowed is 80kmph (50mph). Watch out in the larger towns: Dominican drivers tend to behave with complete disregard of the highway code, changing lanes without indicating (indicators are often missing), riding mopeds down one-way streets in the wrong direction, slamming on the brakes of their minibuses if they spot their passengers too late, etc. Drivers from abroad would be advised to travel with caution and always stay alert. Eye contact is the best communication. Traveling by night should be avoided.

Hire cars

Sleepy streets

The main car rental firms have offices at the major airports and in the larger towns and tourist centers. A driving li-

cence and credit card usually have to be provided; without them it takes quite a bit of persuasion to obtain a car, and a large deposit needs to be paid. Be sure to ask about insurance regulations, otherwise things can become very expensive if an accident does occur.

Hiring motorbikes is a risky business. Many rental firms won't insure you. In the tourist centers, bikes and mopeds are often stolen.

By air

The national airline Air Santo Domingo offers scheduled air connections to popular tourist destinations within the Dominican Republic several times daily. For further information, tel: 683 8020.

By bus

The main towns are easily reached by bus. Buses in the Dominican Republic are comfortable and many of them have air-conditioning, too. The three largest bus companies are Metro, Caribe Tours and Compañía de Autobuses. Visitors are recommended to reserve seats in advance.

By 'guagua'

On lesser roads, smaller buses known as *guaguas* are more common. These can be boarded in the central squares of most villages, or hailed with a wave from the roadside. The problem is, most *guaguas* are jam-packed with passengers. Seen in a positive light, however, it's a great way of meeting people.

Guagua

By pick-up

Another form of transportation is the pick-up; passengers simply sit in the open back.

Pick-up ride

By públicos and motoconchos

The *Carros Públicos* (or *Conchos*), cars or minibuses that function as shared taxis, can be found in all the larger towns. To get a ride, just stand at the roadside and signal to the driver. The *Públicos* travel along fixed routes, but those unfamiliar with the area should always check them with a map first.

The cheapest form of motorized transportation, very much in evidence on the north coast, are the mopeds or *motoconchos*. It's not uncommon to see up to three or even four people plus the rider sitting on these. Decide on the fare in advance.

By taxi

Taxis are far more expensive than *Públicos*. The half-hour trip from the airport to the center of Santo Domingo costs about US$20–30.

Souvenirs galore in La Romana

Facts for the Visitor

Travel documents

For stays not exceeding three months, a passport valid for at least six months is necessary. In addition, visitors from the US and Canada require a tourist card, which is valid for 90 days and costs US$10. It can be purchased from consulates, tourist offices, airlines on departure or at the airport on arrival.

Local brands

Customs regulations

Visitors to the Dominican Republic are allowed to bring in 1 liter of alcohol, 200 cigarettes and presents to the value of US$100. If you have any expensive cameras, computers, or cassette players, make sure you convince the customs officers that they are for your own personal use and will be taken with you when you leave. If you let the officials make a note of the appliances in your passport there should be no problem.

The airport police are on the lookout for illegal drugs. It is also illegal to bring firearms into the country.

Tourist information
In the US
Dominican Republic Tourist Board, 136 E 57th Street, Suite 803, New York, NY 10022, tel: 212-588 1012, fax: 588 1015, email: dr.info@ix.netcom; 2355 Salzedo Street, Suite 305, Coral Gables, Miami, Florida 33134, tel: 305-444 4592, fax: 444 4845, email: domrep@herald.infi.net.
In the UK
Dominican Republic Tourist Board, 18–20 Hand Court, High Holborn, London WC1V 6JF, tel: 020 7242 7778, fax: 020 7405 4202. Or alternatively visit the Dominican Republic's website: http.//www.dominican-rep.com.

In the Dominican Republic

Secretaria de Estado de Turismo (Department of Tourism), Avenida México, tel: 1-809 221 4660, 1-200-3500 (toll-free in Dominican Republic), fax: 1-809 682 3806. Puerto Plata, tel: 1-809 586 3676.

Dirección Nacional de Parques (National Park Administration), Avenida Máximo Gómez, Cementerio Antiguo, Santo Domingo, tel: 1-809 472 4204, fax: 1-809 472 4012.

Ecoturisa, Santo Domingo, tel: 1-809 221 4104, fax: 1-809 685 1544.

Marina (CIBINA), University of Santo Domingo, tel: 1-809 544 2812.

Fundacion Dominicana por Investigacion y Conservacion de los Recursos Marinos, Avenida Anacoana 77, Santo Domingo, tel: 1-809 686 3250.

Sauntering in Sosúa

Airline offices in Santo Domingo

Alitalia, Edificio in Tempo, Local 202, Avenida Winston Churchill, tel: 1-809 562 1767.

Air France, Avenida George Washington 101, tel: 1-809 686 8412/8419.

ALM, Leopoldo Navarro 28, tel: 1-809 687 4569.

American Airlines: Edificio in Tempo, 4th floor, Avenida Winston Churchill, tel: 1-809 542 5151.

American Eagle (to San Juan, Puerto Rico), Edificio Las Brisas 60, Juan Sánchez Ramírez, tel: 1-809 682 0077.

Apa Internacional Air, Avenida de Febrero 27, Tiradentes, tel: 1-809 547 2727.

Caces, Gustavo Mejía Ricart 93, tel: 1-809 541 5151.

Continental, Edificio in Tempo, Avenida Winston Churchill, tel: 809-541 2000. Airport, tel: 1-809 562 6688.

Copa Airlines, Edificio in Tempo, Avenida Winston Churchill, tel: 1-809 562 5824.

Iberia, El Conde 401, tel: 1-809 686 9191.

Lufthansa, Avenida George Washington 353, tel: 1-809 689 9625.

TAP Air Portugal, Avenida de Febrero 27, Tiradentes, tel: 1-809 472 1441/549 0021/549 0104.

Viasa, Avenida de Febrero 27, Tiradentes, tel: 1-809 472 1492.

87

Currency and exchange

Pesos

The official unit of currency in the Dominican Republic is the *peso* (RD$), equivalent to 100 *centavos*. There are 5, 10, 20, 50, 100, 500 and 1,000 peso banknotes, and it's always best to have a few 5 and 10 peso notes handy for excursions and *guagua* rides (*see page 85*), because larger notes can't usually be changed.

It is best to take US dollars in cash or as traveler's checks, because exchanging them is no problem. Mastercard, Visa and Amex are the most commonly accepted credit cards. Visitors are advised to exchange money at hotels or in banks as black market transactions are illegal. Beware of confidence tricksters.

Import or export of the local currency is forbidden. However, there is no limit on the amount of foreign currency that can be brought into the Dominican Republic.

Tipping
In hotels a 21 percent surcharge is levied on the basic price, composed of 11 percent tax for the room and 10 percent for service. An additional 8 percent tax is also charged on meals in restaurants, plus another 10 percent service charge. However, it's still customary to express your satisfaction by leaving a 5–10 percent gratuity as well.

Opening times
Banks
8.30am–3pm, closed Saturday and Sunday.
Stores
Monday to Friday, 8am–7pm. Some stores are open on Saturday and Sunday morning.

88

Post offices close at 5pm

Post offices
8am–5pm, closed Sunday.
Government offices
7.30am–2.30pm, closed Saturday and Sunday.
Private offices (and some stores)
8.30am–12.30pm and 2.30–6.30pm, closed Saturday and Sunday.
Museums and places of interest
Closed Monday. The official times aren't always precise, and are often subject to change for no apparent reason.

Taíno art

Public holidays
1 January (New Year's Day), 6 January (Epiphany), 21 January (Festival of Our Lady of Altagracia, the country's patron saint), 26 January (*Día de Duarte*, the birthday of Juan P. Duarte, the founder of the Republic), 27 February (*Día de la Independencia*, National Independence Day), March–April (*Semana Santa*, Good Friday and Easter Sunday), May (Ascension, Corpus Christi), 1 May (Labor Day), 15 August (Assumption of the Virgin), 16 August (Restoration Day), 24 September (Day of Patron Saint Nuestra Señora de las Mercedes), 12 October (*Día de la Raza*, Columbus Day), November (All Saints' Day), 25 December (Christmas Day).

Flag waving

Postal services
The postal service is very slow. It is best not to put your mail in the rather unreliable post boxes, but to pay a little extra for *entrega especial* (special delivery) for which post offices have a separate window.

Telephone

Domestic and international calls can be made from most places; use a phone in a Codetel center (recognisable by the blue-and-orange logo). Dial the number you want and an operator will ask for the name of the party you require plus the number of the booth you're in (in Spanish or in English). You pay when you leave (credit cards are accepted); for telephone boxes you need 25 centavo coins. AT&T's USA-Direct is available on 1-800-872 2881. If calling from one place to another on the island always dial 1 before the number. For the UK dial 01144, followed by the area code (minus its initial zero) and then the number itself. The Codetel offices also have a fax service, and it's worth remembering that faxes are often far cheaper than phone calls. Another tip: the rates charged by the TRI-COM phone company are more competitive than those charged by Codetel.

Local news

Newspapers, radio, television

Six morning papers and three evening ones provide up-to-date information: *Listín Diario, El Caribe, El Nuevo Diario, El Siglo, El Sol, Hoy, El Nacional, La Noticia* and *Ultima Hora*. There are also three newspapers in English: the *Santo Domingo News* (and also the *Puerto Plata News*), *Touring* and *Hispaniola Business*. The Dominican Republic has 179 radio stations and 10 television channels. Most hotels can receive American cable TV.

About town

Clothing

Neatness is very important to the Dominicans. Even the poorest will invest much of the little they have in looking presentable. Any tourist who walks through the streets wearing flip-flops, tight swimming trunks and a scanty T-shirt is considered stupid, and offends the aesthetic sense of the locals. Swimming things should thus be kept close to the beach. At other times it's best to wear light clothing made of cotton or other natural fibers; take a pullover for cooler evenings and rainwear in case of tropical downpours. For hikes in the mountains and national parks, sturdy footwear is essential.

Souvenirs

Shopping in the Dominican Republic is most appreciated by people who don't mind haggling. The locals are experts at this. The most popular purchases include jewelry made of amber, turquoise-colored larimar, gold, or silver.

One of the opening scenes of Steven Spielberg's film *Jurassic Park* was set in the Dominican Republic and shows a 100 million-year-old insect found trapped in amber in a quarry. The story goes that just before it died it had

Paintings make a good souvenir

sucked blood from a dinosaur, and the tiny drop of blood from its stomach provided enough DNA information for scientists to bring dinosaurs back to life... Well, the Dominican Republic does indeed have rich supplies of amber – that much is true. It's a fossil tree resin that occurs in all shades of yellow with nuances of orange and brown. Deeply colored transparent amber is highly prized as gem material and is used to make necklaces, rings and armbands. The leaves, ants or spiders it contains, some of them several million years old, provide fascinating information on the way the earth's flora and fauna have evolved.

Beware not to purchase articles made of black coral or tortoiseshell, for ecological reasons as well as your own safety: trading in or exporting these materials is strictly forbidden, as is importing them to the US and most European countries.

It's impossible to miss the colorful paintings in all shapes and sizes exhibited by Haitians in all the tourist areas. Wickerwork, leather goods, wood carvings, machetes, carnival masks and the famous *muñeca sin rostro* (faceless clay dolls) from the region around Moca are good buys. Hand-rolled cigars also make traditional souvenirs; for some years now they have been produced under the supervision of the firm 'Davidoff'.

Photography

Photographic material, especially slide film, can only be purchased in the larger tourist centers or in hotel stores, and is often overpriced. Dominicans generally don't mind having their photos taken, but it's best to ask first.

Time Zones

The Dominican Republic has Atlantic Standard Time (AST), which is Central European Time minus five hours. During European summer time the difference is six hours.

Voltage

The voltage in the Dominican Republic is 110v, and the sockets fit American plugs. There are quite a few power outages *(apagones)*, especially in the evenings when consumption is high. Many hotels have their own generators *(plantas)* to handle the situation. It could well prove useful, however, to carry a torch and/or a candle in your luggage.

Medical

No particular vaccinations are necessary for a trip to the Dominican Republic, though protection against tetanus, polio and hepatitis A is probably a good idea. Malaria precautions are not generally required unless you are planning to spend some time in the border region close to Haiti.

The best way to prevent any stomach or bowel complaints is to drink only pure water *(agua purificada)*, sold in plastic bottles, and to avoid ice cubes, ice cream, fresh salads and fruit juices mixed with water.

It's best to take out some kind of health insurance before going to the Dominican Republic. Make sure transportation back home is also included in the cover in case of severe illness.

The health system in the Dominican Republic is generally very good. Most towns have their own doctors and clinics, and tourist centers always do. Payment has to be made immediately following treatment; receipts are provided. Down-payments have to be made for hospital stays.

Insects

The cockroaches *(cuacarachas)* can sometimes be as long as a human finger; they may look disgusting, but they're not at all dangerous to humans. The mosquitoes are another story: they can be troublesome during the evening, despite the people with spray devices who rush round the tourist hotels. Even worse than mosquitoes are the buffalo gnats *(jejenes)* that hover close to the ground. Fly sprays are only of limited use here, so wear trousers, socks and a long-sleeved T-shirt when dusk falls. In some areas, mosquito nets *(mosquitero)* will come in handy; they're available on request from every hotel.

Emergencies

For ambulance, police and the fire department dial 911 anywhere in the country.

Call 771 in Santo Domingo

Crime

Many people have a false impression of crime levels in Third-World countries. The crime rate in the Dominican Republic is far lower than that of most European countries, and outside the tourist centers it's relatively safe. The main holiday centers have to cope with prostitution, drug smuggling and black marketeering. Keep an eye on your documents and personal possessions and avoid dangerous situations (eg remote beaches at dusk, shady bars and neighborhoods). The larger hotels have a safe for valuables. Never leave your luggage or any valuables in your rental car.

Diplomatic Representation

US Embassy and Consulate, Avenida César Nicolás Penson, Santo Domingo, tel: embassy, 221 2171; consulate, 221 5511.

British Embassy and Consulate, Avenida 27 de Febrero, 233, 7th Floor, Santo Domingo, tel: 472 7111; fax: 472 7574.

Accommodation

The Dominican Republic has various types of accommodation: 'tourist hotels' conform to international standards, come in various price categories and often have their own restaurant or nightclub attached; 'aparthotels' have self-catering facilities and are useful for longer stays; 'boarding houses' range from spartan to very comfortable and so does the service. The latter are the cheapest, though prices for the simplest accommodation fluctuate wildly depending on the region.

In the Dominican Republic itself, information on accommodation can be obtained from Tourist Information at Santo Domingo International Airport, and there is also an information office on the Malecón (harbor promenade) in Puerto Plata. For descriptions of accommodation it's well worth looking at English-language newspapers such as the *Santo Domingo News,* the *Puerto Plata News* or *Touring*.

Only the very courageous – who don't mind a disappointment – would be advised to follow the people who can sometimes be seen hanging round the airport waving color photographs of 'exclusive bungalows right next to the sea'; the photos don't always reflect the reality all that accurately!

The best way to find accommodation in the smaller resorts is to sit in one of the cafés and simply ask the locals or the tourists there.

By the way, a word of warning: 'motels' very often turn out to be brothels.

Hotel Selection

The following suggestions from the main centers are listed according to three categories: $$$ = expensive; $$ = moderate; $ = inexpensive.

Azua de Compostela
$Altagracia, Calle Duarte 59, tel: 521 3286. **$Brisas del Mar**, Calle de Leones, tel: 521 3813.

Baní
$$Los Almendros, Playa Los Almendros. **$Caribani**, Calle Sánchez, tel: 522 4400. **$Brisas del Sur**, tel: 522 2548.

Barahona
$$Riviera Beach, Avenida Enriquillo 56, tel: 524 5111, fax: 524 5798. **$Caribe**, Avenida Enriquillo, tel: 524 2185. **$Hotel Guaracuyá**, Saladilla, tel: 524-2211. **$Barahona**, Calle Jaime Mora 5, tel: 524 3442. **$Victoria**, Padre Bellini 15-A, tel: 542 2392.

The Palacio, best hotel in Santo Domingo

Tourist hotel

Hostal Nicolás de Nader

Boca Chica
$$$Coral Hamaca, Calle Duarte, tel: 523 4611, fax: 523 6767. **$$$Don Juan Beach Resort**, tel: 523 4511, fax: 688 5271. **$Vista Tropical**, Calle Duarte 73, tel: 523 4763.

The Hamaca

Cabarete
$$Camino del Sol, tel: 571 0893. **$Casa Laguna**, tel: 571 0725, fax: 571 0704.

Higüey
$Brisas del Este, Avenida Mella, tel: 554 2112. **$Don Carlos**, Calle Ponce de León, tel: 554 2344.

Juan Dolio
$$$Casa Marina Talanquera Beach Resort, tel: 526 1510, fax: 526 2408. **$$Barceló Capella Beach Resort**, tel: 526 1080. **$$Tamarindo Sunclub**, tel: 412 2001.

La Romana
$$$Casa de Campo. Holiday village on eastern outskirts, tel: 523 3333, fax: 523 8548. **$Frano**, Avenida Padre Abreu 9, tel: 550 4744. **$Adamaney**, 556 6102.

93

La Vega
$$Guaricano, Carretera Duarte, tel: 573 2632.

Las Terrenas
$$$Cacao Beach, tel: 240 6000, fax: 240 6020. **$$El Portillo Beach Club**, tel: 688 5717, fax: 685 0547. **$$Atlantis**, Punta Bonita, tel: 240 6111, fax: 240 6205. **$Coyamar**, Playa Bonita, tel/fax: 248 2353. **$Acaya**, Playa Bonita, tel: 240 6161, fax: 240 6166.

The Atlantis

Luperón
$$Luperon Beach Resort, Cd Marina, tel: 581 4153, fax: 581 6262.

Monte Cristi
$Cabañas Las Carabelas, on the road to El Morro, tel: 579 2682. **$Chic**, Benito Monción 44, tel: 579 2316.

Puerto Plata
$$$Victoria, tel: 320 1200, fax: 320 4862. **$$$Paradise Beach Club**, tel: 562 7475, fax: 566 2436. For the young. **$$$Gran Venana**, tel:320 2111, fax: 230 2112. All inclusive holiday village at the beach. **$$Montemar**, Calle Hermanas Mirabal, tel: 320 2800, fax: 320 2009. With sea view. **$$Cofresí**, Playa Cofresí, tel: 586 2898, fax: 586 1828. **$Hostal Jimesson**, Calle John F Kennedy 41, tel: 586 5131, fax: 586 6313. Cheap but graceful living in a 100-year-old merchant's house.

Samaná
$$$Cayacoa, tel: 538 3131, fax: 538 2985. **$$$Cayo Levantado Beach Resort**, tel: 538 2988, 223 8704 (in Santo Domingo), fax: 538 2985. **$Tropical Lodge**, at the eastern end of Malecón, tel: 538 2480, fax: 538 2046.

San Cristóbal
$Constitución, Avenida Constitución 118, tel: 528 3309. **$San Cristóbal**, Anenida Libertad 32, tel: 528 3555.

San Pedro de Macorís
$Macorís Uce, G Deligne, tel: 529 3950. **$Nuevo Central**, Calle San Francisco 49, tel: 588 2304. **$Altagracia**, Avenida Libertad 1332, tel: 588 6470.

Santiago de los Caballeros
$$$Camino Real, Calle del Sol, corner of Calle Mella, tel: 581 7000, fax: 582 4566. **$$$Hotel Gran Almirante**, Avenida Estrella Sadhalá, Los Jardines, tel: 580 1992, fax: 241 1492. **$$Ahloa Sol**, Calle del Sol 50, tel: 583 0090, fax: 583 0950. **$Mercedes**, Calle 30 Marzo 18, tel: 583 1171, fax: 581 5207.

The V Centenario and Jaragua

Santo Domingo
$$$Ramada Renaissance Jaragua Resort, tel: 221 2222, fax: 686 0528. **$$$ V Centenario**, tel: 221 0000, fax: 221 2020. **$$$El Embajador**, Avda. Sarasota 65, tel: 221 2131, fax: 532 5306. Large, well-maintained hotel in beautiful grounds, with swimming pool. **$$$Santo Domingo**, corner of Calle Independencia and Avenida Lincoln, tel: 221 1511, fax: 535 1511. Swimming pool, night club, sauna. **$$Nicolas de Ovando,** Calle Las Damas 53 (Zona Colonial), tel: 687 3101, fax: 688 5170. Former governor's house, historic atmosphere. **$$Palacio**, Calle Duarte 106, tel: 682 4730, fax: 687 5535. Spanish-colonial-style hotel, small and attractive, run by Germans. **$$Naco**, Calle Tradentes 22, tel: 562 3100, fax: 544 0957. **$$Plaza del Sol**, Calle José Contreras 25, tel: 687 1317. Self-catering apartments. **$$Drake**, Calle Augustin Lara 29, tel: 567 4427. Self-catering apartments.**$$Francés**, Calle Las Mercedes, corner Calle Arzobispo Meriño, tel: 685 9331, fax: 685 1289. Small hotel in colonial building. **$El Señorial**, Calle Presidente Vicini Burgon 58, tel: 687 4359, fax: 689 0600. Near old town. **$El Napolitano**, Malecón, tel: 687 1131, fax: 689 2714.

Solitude in Sosúa

Sosúa
$$$Sand Castle Beach Resort, Puerto Chiquito, tel: 571 2420, fax: 571 2000. **$$Playa Chiquita**, tel: 571 3416. **$Sea Breeze**, Calle Dr A Martínez, tel: 571 3858, fax: 571 2115. **$Sosúa Ocean Front Guest House**, tel: 571 2284.

Index

Administration 7
Alpes Dominicanos 54
Altos de Chavón 68
Amber Coast 39–44
Azua de
  Compostela........59–60

Balneario La
  Confluencia 54
Baní........................58
Barahona 60–1
Bávaro Beach Resort...70
Bayahibe 69
Boca Chica 66
Boca de Yuma 70
Bonao 55

Cabarete 43
Cabo Francés Viejo
  National Park..........43
carnival.....................75
Cayo Levantado 44
climate.......................6
cockfighting...............75
Columbus, Christopher
  ......14, 15, 38, 46, 53
Constanza.................55
cuisine 77–8

Deep sea fishing....70, 81
Descubierta 64
diving 80

Economy 7–8
education 11
El Limón 44
environment 8–9

Fortaleza Nuestra
  Señora de la
  Concepción 54

Goulouyas dances ...67, 75

Haitians 11
Hatillo 59
Hato Mayor 70–1
Higüey.....................70
hiking 81
history 14–15

Isla Cabritos 64
Isla Saona 69

Jarabacoa 54
Jaragua National Park .62
Jimaní.....................64
Juan Dolio 66

La Caleta 65–6
La Isabela 46
La Romana 67–8
La Vega....................53
La Vega Vieja 53
Laguna del Rincón 64
Laguna Estero Hondo .47
Laguna Gri Gri...........43
Lake Enriquillo 63–4
landscape................5–6
Las Caritas caves....63–4
Las Salinas
  Peninsula 58
Las Terrenas 43–4
Los Haïtises
  National Park....44, 71
Luperón 45

Merengue music 73–4
Miches 71
Mirabal sisters........51–2
Moca 51
Monte Cristi
  National Park..........48
Museo de las
  Hermanas Mirabal 52
Museo del Ambar
  Dominicano 40–1
Museo del Tabaco .49–50
Museo Folklórico
  de Tomás Morel 50
Museo Panteón...........66

Nagua 43
Najayo beach..........57–8
Neiba 63
Nigua 57

Palmar de Ocoa 59
Paraíso 61
Parque Nacional
  Monte Cristi............48
Parque Submarino 66
  Pedernales 62
people 10
Pico Duarte...............54
Pico Isabel de
  Torres 40, 42
Playa Grande 43
Playa Baní 58
Playa San Rafael 61
politics.......................7
Puerto Plata 39–41
Puerto Viejo 60
Punta Rucia 47

Restaurants...............79
Río San Juan 43

Sabana de la Mar 71
Salcedo 51–2
Salto de Baiguate 54
Salto de Jimenoa 54
Samaná 44
San Cristóbal 56–7
San José de Ocoa 59
San Juan de Maguana..60
San Pedro de Macorís .67
San Rafael de
  Yuma 69–70
Sánchez 43
Santiago de los
  Caballeros.........49–51
Santo Cerro 53
Santo Domingo 18–38
  Acuario Nacional......38
  Alcázar de Colón 24
  Atarazanas 25
  Avenida Duarte 33
  Basílica Menor 20–1
  Calle El Conde 31
  Calle las Damas........22
  Calle La Regina 29
  Capilla de la
    Tercera Orden 29
  Capilla del Rosario 37
  Casa de Bastidas........23
  Casa de Francia 23
  Casa de la Moneda 26
  Casa de los Jesuitas 24
  Casa de Tostado 28
  Casa del Cordón 26
  Casas Reales 24
  Centro de los Héroes 35
  Church of Regina
    Angelorum............29
  Church of San
    Lázaro 33
  Church of Santa
    Clara....................22
  Colegio de Gorjón 29
  Convento de los
    Dominicos.............29
  Convento San
    Francisco..............27
  Faro a Colón 37–8
  Fortaleza Ozama...22–3
  Galería del Arte
    Moderno...............34
  Hospital San
    Nicolás de Bari 27
  Hospital Padre
    Billini 32
  Hostal Nicolás de
    Ovando.................23
  Iglesia Conventual
    de las Mercedes 33

Iglesia del Carmen....31
Iglesia Santa
  Bárbara..................26
Jardin Botánico.........36
Juan Pablo Duarte
  Museum 26
Los Tres Ojos 38
Malecón, the 30
Mercado Modelo 33
Monumento a
  Montesino 30
Museo del Hombre
  Dominicano 34
Museo de la Familia
  Dominicana............28
Museo de las
  Atarazanas Reales ..25
Museo de las
  Casas Reales 24
Museo de la Historia
  y Geografía 34
Old Town Hall..........27
Orchid Park 36
Palacio de Bellas
  Artes.....................35
Palacio de
  Borgellá 22
Palacio Nacional........36
Panteón Nacional......23
Parque Colón ...20, 28
Parque de la
  Cultura 33–5
Parque de la
  Independencia 30–1
Parque del Este 38
Parque Mirador
  del Sur...................36
Parque Zoológico 36
Plaza Arqueología
  la Ceiba 25–6
Plaza España..............25
Plaza Padre Billini 28
Puerta de la
  Misericordia...........30
Puerta de San Diego .24
Puerta del Conde 30
Puerta San José.........29
Sosúa......................42
sugar mills 57, 67–8

Taíno Indians.....12–13,
  53, 63–4, 73
Trinitaria, La 14, 31–2

Voodoo 12

Whales 44
Windsurfing 42, 80–1